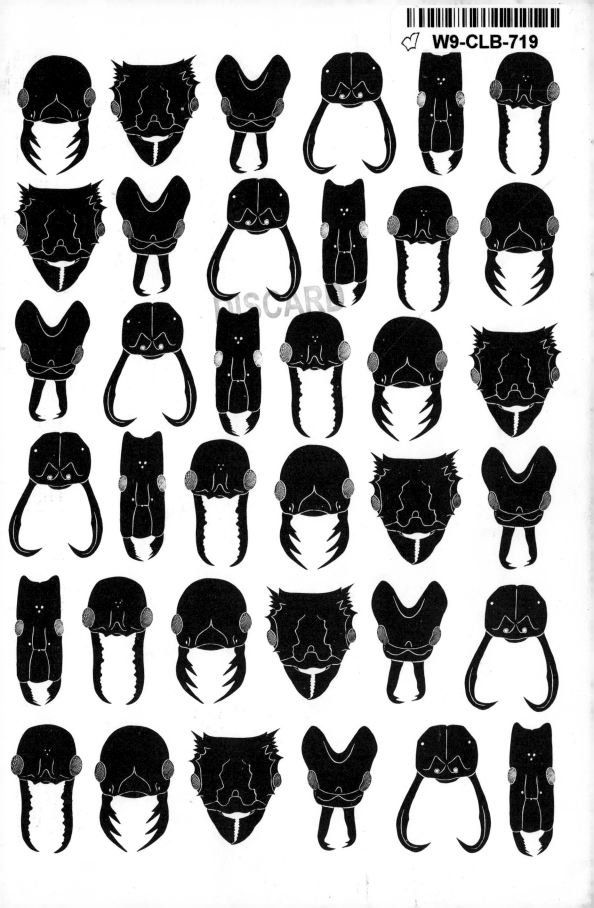

W9-CLB-719

IDENTIFICATION OF ANT HEADS SHOWN ON END SHEETS. Top row, left to right: *Thaumatomyrmex*, a primitive ant of Brazil; *Acromyrmex*, a fungus-growing ant of South America; *Daceton*, a jumping ant of South America; *Eciton*, an army ant of Central and South America; *Leptomyrmex*, a native of Australia; *Myrmecia*, a bulldog ant of Australia.

The Ant Realm

Other Books by Ross E. Hutchins

THE AMAZING SEEDS

CADDIS INSECTS: NATURE'S CARPENTERS AND STONEMASONS

INSECT BUILDERS AND CRAFTSMEN

INSECTS

INSECTS—HUNTERS AND TRAPPERS

LIVES OF AN OAK TREE

PLANTS WITHOUT LEAVES

STRANGE PLANTS AND THEIR WAYS

THIS IS A FLOWER

THIS IS A LEAF

THIS IS A TREE

THE TRAVELS OF MONARCH X

WILD WAYS: A BOOK OF ANIMAL HABITS

The Ant Realm

ROSS E. HUTCHINS

Photographs by the Author

Dodd, Mead & Company · New York

FRONTISPIECE: *A carpenter ant*

All photographs are by the author except those
on pages 43, 183, and 195.

To Allen Puckett
for so many reasons

Introduction

IF YOU WERE to ask a biologist which of all the so-called lower animals he considered to be closest to man in habits, he would probably say the ants. This might come as a surprise to you since ants are not at all closely related to us but belong to the great host of backboneless creatures known as Arthropods or joint-legged animals. To this same group also belong other insects, as well as crabs, spiders, and crayfishes.

The ants are an ancient tribe; they came into being at about the same time in geological history as the first mammals or hairy animals. This was during the Mesozoic, a period which began nearly 200 million years ago when the world's climates were warm and semi-arid.

The ants are thus far older than the human race and their "civilizations" were well developed long before our primitive ancestors stood up and walked on two legs. Even then, the ants had skilled "trades" which set them apart from all other creatures. The first ants were hunters that preyed upon other insects, then they settled down in permanent colonies and became farmers, seed-gatherers and herdsmen. Some kinds, then as now, enslaved other ants to do their work. They evolved police forces or soldiers to protect their "cities" from enemies, and young worker ants passed through stages of apprenticeship or training. Between the ways of ants and men there is, however, a great basic difference: ants do their particular work by instinct or inherited "knowledge" while each of us usually learns a trade or profession.

Of all the world's insects, the ants are probably the most remarkable when we consider their amazing habits and the ways in which these resemble our own. This is the story of the strange and fascinating realm of the ants.

R. E. H.

Contents

Introduction   vii

1. THE SOCIAL INSECTS   1

2. THE ANT WORLD   15

3. THE HUNTERS   39

4. THE WARRIOR ANTS   50

5. THE SEED GATHERERS   70

6. THE MUSHROOM GROWERS   87

7. THE HONEY ANTS   110

8. THE HERDSMEN   123

9. THE SLAVE-MAKERS   132

10. ANTS AND THEIR TREES   138

11. GUESTS AND FIFTH COLUMNISTS   158

12. OF WAR AND PEACE   171

13. ANTS IN AMBER   180

14. THE TERMITE CLAN   188

A Selected Bibliography   199

Index   201

Yellowjackets are typical social insects. They construct paper nests in underground cavities where the colony of hot-tempered insects lives. Such a colony consists of a queen and hundreds of workers, all of which are her daughters. Only the mated queens survive the winter to establish new colonies in spring.

Chapter 1

The Social Insects

THE STUDY of any insects can be fascinating, but those that live in colonies which, in a general way, resemble human cities are certainly the most interesting of all. This social habit is found among many insects, including ants, bees, wasps, hornets, and termites. Most other insects are non-social; that is, the females lay their eggs on or near sources of food and then leave, having no further interest in them or the young which hatch from them. This is the state of things in the case of grasshoppers, butterflies, moths, and most other insects. The next step up the social ladder is found among those insects in which the female constructs a special nest for her future offspring. She does not remain with them to give them any sort of care but she does build some kind of nest stocked with proper food. A good example of this is found among the solitary wasps such as the mud-daubers and hunting wasps. In the case of mud-daubers, the female builds a clay cell, stocks it with spiders she has paralyzed by her sting and, after laying an egg, seals the cell with more clay. She may then leave the vicinity or begin the construction of another cell. In the meantime, the egg in the cell hatches and the larval wasp begins feeding on the paralyzed spiders. When fully grown the larva changes into the pupal or resting stage and, in time, the adult, winged wasp emerges and gnaws its way out of the cell. But the mother wasp has left and never sees her offspring. The hunting wasps that excavate nests in the ground and stock them with paralyzed grasshoppers, cicadas, horseflies, or other "game," have similar life histories.

On the next rung up the social ladder of insects we come to those in which the female remains with her eggs until they hatch and then cares for her young until they are able to shift for themselves. This commendable habit occurs among a number of insects, including some stinkbugs, a few beetles, and several cockroaches. There is a stinkbug or Pentatomid *(Mecistorhinus tripterus)* found on cacao in Trinidad that lays her cylindrical eggs in a cluster and guards them until they hatch. The mother bug remains with her offspring for a time, perhaps giving them some protection. I once saw a similar bug deep in the Everglades convoying her young along the limb of a gumbo limbo tree. This sub-social habit is also found in most earwigs (order *Dermaptera)*. In such insects we see the beginnings of definite social habits. In autumn, a mated pair of earwigs excavates a small cavity in the ground and remains there until spring. At this time the female drives her mate out of the nest and then lays her eggs. When the young hatch, they are protected by the female during at least a portion of their immature lives. Later, the young are on their own, and there is no continuation of family life.

At the top of the social ladder we come to the true social insects, the elite of the six-footed clan. Here are found the honeybees, the hornets,

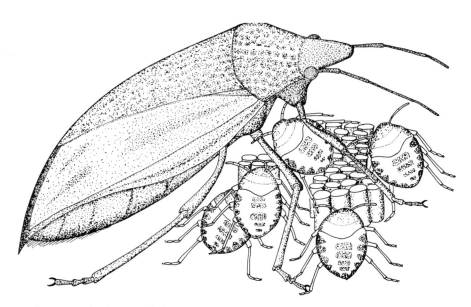

*In this West Indian stink-bug (*Mecistorhinus*) we find the beginnings of the social habit. After laying her can-shaped eggs, the female guards them until they hatch and then remains with the young for several days. This protects them from enemies.*

2

Ant colonies often consist of thousands of workers, as in this imported fire ant mound. Usually, there is but one queen. Winged males are present only at certain seasons.

ants, and termites. Among these insects, we find that large colonies or families are the rule. We may speak of them as "families" with some truth since all the individuals are usually related, having hatched from eggs laid by one queen mother. In the case of termites, however, there may be other egg-laying individuals besides the queen; still, they usually are all related to each other.

Probably the best examples, as well as most interesting of these true social insects, are found among the ant tribes. Ant colonies or "cities" have far more in common with our own metropolitan areas than most people realize. A typical ant nest or colony is usually made up of a mixed population of ants fitted to carry out various duties in connection with colonial or "city" life. While these various individuals do not function or work in the same way as do their human counterparts, the end results are more or less the same. A human city is governed by a mayor and a city council which might, in a very broad way, be compared to the queen ant. But the queen ant does not really "govern" her subjects in the sense that human city officials do. She makes no rules or laws and issues no orders, yet her influence is felt throughout the

3

Queen ants are usually larger than their workers. Here is (left) a queen carpenter ant and (right) a worker with a few eggs which have been laid by the queen.

Ants communicate with each other by means of their sensitive antennae. On meeting, they often touch antennae and apparently exchange information. Shown here are two carpenter ants (Camponotus) in the act of touching antennae.

colony as a result of certain chemical substances which are secreted by her and passed out to the workers. This, in the case of honeybees is called the "queen substance" and, while the queen is alive, it is circulated continuously among all the workers from mouth to mouth. In effect, this is a chemical message that controls and regulates many of the activities within the hive. This trading, or passing around, of glandular secretions is very common among social insects and is called *trophallaxis*. It accounts for many activities of these insects that might, at first, appear to be intelligent or instinctive acts. Since honeybees have been studied much more than ants, we know much more about their social life than we do about that of ants. If a queen honeybee is killed, the entire colony down to the last worker is soon aware of the fact. This is because the supply of "queen substance" secreted continually by her and passed along from worker to worker is cut off. When this occurs, the bees soon become disturbed and do not work. They seem to "know" that without their queen the hive is doomed because she alone, of all the bees in the colony, is capable of laying worker eggs. Within a few weeks, especially in summer, the colony will cease to exist because the life of a worker bee is but a short time.

Not only does this "queen substance" control the activities of the

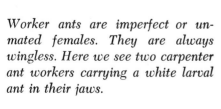

Worker ants are imperfect or unmated females. They are always wingless. Here we see two carpenter ant workers carrying a white larval ant in their jaws.

worker bees but it influences the development of their glands as well. When the queen becomes old, the supply of "queen substance" she secretes changes in character or becomes less in amount. As a result, the workers construct queen cells in each of which the queen lays a fertilized egg. A new queen develops in each of these cells. If the queen dies, the ovaries of some of the workers begin developing and these individuals eventually begin laying eggs. However, since these workers have not mated, all their eggs will hatch into drones, since only drones result from non-fertilized eggs.

In a general way, the social life of ants is similar to that of bees and hornets, which is not surprising when we remember that all these insects are quite closely related. An ant colony, like a bee hive, is a female society or matriarchy. It consists of a queen, many workers and, perhaps, some soldiers, all of which are females. There are, of course, male ants but these are lesser in number and not always present in the colony. Male ants correspond to the drones in a colony of honeybees.

In the case of honeybees, a new colony or hive arises as a result of swarming. When swarming, the queen bee leaves the parent colony, taking a few hundred workers with her. This swarm settles on a tree

Larval ants are white and grublike. Being helpless at this stage, they are fed and cared for by the worker ants. Notice how small the head of this harvester ant larva is.

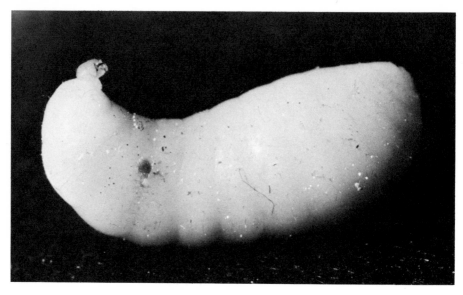

*Young queens have wings but, after the mating flight, these wings are broken off since she will have no further use for them. Shown here is a young carpenter ant queen (*Camponotus*). After mating, she will establish her colony in rotten wood.*

limb and scout bees then go out seeking a satisfactory location for their future home, which may be in a hollow tree or, perhaps, in a hollow porch column. When the scouts agree on the new site, the swarm flies off and sets up housekeeping there. In the case of hornets, only the mated queens survive the winter by hibernating in secluded locations. With the coming of spring, these queens construct small paper nests, each with a few cells in which eggs are laid. The grubs or *larvae* (singular, *larva*) that hatch from the eggs are fed by the queen. She has full responsibility for both hunting for food and in caring for her young. When these larval hornets mature, they are all of the worker caste and, as such, take over the duties of nest building and food gathering. From then on the queen remains at the nest, spending most of her time laying eggs. Hornet nests, such as the large, paper nests one often sees in trees, are used for only one year in our climate; with the coming of autumn all the inhabitants, except the mated queens, die. The end of summer marks the end of the hornet colony. In tropical countries, many hornets and wasps construct nests which remain occupied for several years.

The founding of an ant colony is, in general, rather similar to the establishment of a hornet colony. During most of the year the inhabitants of an ant colony consist only of wingless workers or imperfect females, but at certain seasons, usually in spring, winged male and female ants are produced which swarm out of old colonies. These females or queens mate, either with males from the same or from nearby colonies, the males then die. In the meantime, the mated queens fly away seeking places to establish nests. In many kinds, this is in the ground but others prefer rotten wood or other locations. The queen then severs her wings, either by pulling them off with her legs or jaws or by rubbing them against some object. They appear to be rather easily detached. Wings, during her future life, will be of little use to her so she gets rid of them. After excavating a small cell, she lays a few eggs and, when these hatch, the larvae are fed on material secreted by her. She has a large thorax or midsection filled with flight muscles which are no longer needed since her wings have been severed. These useless muscles are slowly dissolved and converted into nutrients which sustain both queen and young during this period of isolation. Sometimes the queen eats some of her own eggs to help her survive. In time, the larval ants reach maturity and go into the pupal or resting stage and, eventually, the adult worker ants emerge. These first workers

Notice the large thorax or mid-section of this carpenter ant queen. After her mating flight she severed her wings. If you look carefully you can see where they were attached.

Ant pupae are helpless and do not feed. They are cared for by the adult work-ers. Shown here is a pupal harvester ant (Pogonomyrmex).

may be smaller than normal, or midgets, due to the small amounts of food they received during their growth. Once the queen has a few workers to help her, the nest cavity is enlarged and expeditions are made away from the nest to gather food. As time passes, the nest be-comes larger and larger as additional worker ants are produced.

As might be expected, there are many variations in the manner in which these new ant colonies are established. Some queens cannot establish new colonies without the help of workers; they find it neces-sary to take a few workers along when they leave the parent nest, while other queens, such as those of the red wood ant *(Formica rufa)*, return to the parent nest after mating where they join the old queen in the duty of laying eggs. On the other hand, some queens are not above seeking the aid of alien species in establishing their queendoms. Such a queen may seek out a queenless colony of some other species, or kind, of ant and be adopted by it. Here, she begins laying eggs and her larvae are fed and cared for by the foreign ants who seem unaware that these young are not their sisters. Eventually, of course, all of the original workers die off and the queen and her own young have the nest to themselves. Sad to relate, some queens are not above killing the rightful queen and then taking over her egg-laying duties. Even less honorable is the method employed by some ant queens who seek

Red and black carpenter ants (Camponotus) *carrying their larvae.*

out a small, foreign colony, kill all the inhabitants and steal the helpless larvae and pupae. She then cares for these young and, when they are mature, enlists their aid in caring for her own young. Since she lives much longer than the workers, the foreign workers soon die and she and her offspring have a ready-made nest to themselves.

10

Unlike a hornet nest, an ant colony usually exists for several years. In many instances, indeed, an ant colony may thrive for a long while, far beyond the life-span of the original queen. What enables an ant colony to do this is the fact that, as the years pass, newly mated queens may be adopted into the colony. This occurs, for example, in the populous colonies of leaf-cutting ants (*Atta*) of the Tropics. In many cases, the mated queens or, we might say, "married daughters," return at once to the parent nest and aid their queen mother in supplying eggs for the colony. Thus, there may be several ant queens in a nest, a condition that almost never occurs in the case of honeybees. As a matter of fact, a queen honeybee immediately sets upon any rival queen present in the hive and kills her with her sting. This is the only use to which the queen honeybee ever puts her sting.

While the lives of honeybees and hornets follow fixed habits and routines, ants are much more adaptable, often being able to change their habits to fit variations in their habitats. This, no doubt, has been an important factor in enabling them to become as widely distributed and as successful as they have.

The evolution of ant societies has followed a path similar to our own. Human society has passed through six steps or stages in its long climb up from savagery. These stages are as follows: Hunting, Pastoral, Agricultural, Commercial, Industrial, and Intellectual. Our very remote ancestors were at first hunters who lived by hunting wild beasts with spears or arrows. They lived in the Hunting Age. Somewhat later they began domesticating wild animals for food and for their skins. Thus, animal husbandry came into vogue and village life became possible. They then were in the Pastoral Age. From here it was but a short step to cultivating crops both to feed the domesticated animals and to produce food for the villagers. Thus began the Agricultural Age. This new way of life brought about other changes. Trade between villages began; crops which would grow in one locality, and which might not grow as well in another, could be exchanged to the mutual benefit of widely separated settlements. Thus, the Age of Commerce began and, in time, this commerce reached across oceans and seas.

Village and city life, as well as expanding populations, eventually brought into being the next stage of human advancement, the Indus-

All ants are considered to be social insects since they live together in colonies where the workers care for their queen and for the young ants. This is a colony of little black ants (Monomorium minimum) with the worker ants caring for the white larval and pupal ants.

trial Age. There gradually grew up manufacturing centers, where things useful to human society could be made for sale or barter. As the nations of the world grew powerful these manufactured products could easily be transported from continent to continent as well as from city to city. All this was stimulated by man's rapidly increasing intellect and by the knowledge that was slowly accumulating. This is the period of history in which we find ourselves today. Actually, we are just at the beginning of the Intellectual Age, the period of world history in which the acquiring of useful knowledge is the primary concern. This is the end result of all the human progress that has gone before and, as far as we know now, all that remains is the acquiring of more and more knowledge and its application to progress and the betterment of mankind.

Long ago, the first primitive ants were probably non-social; that is, they lived as individuals as do the more primitive wasps. The first social ants were hunters that lived by capturing and eating other insects. Dr. W. M. Wheeler, who was the world's foremost authority on ants, calls attention to such ants as *Formica rufa* which live by hunting. These active ants are found in woods and their colonies are small. Their social habits are not very well developed and they do not capture their game by mass attack; each individual ant of the colony hunts by itself and engages in lone combat with other insects. Still, there are no completely non-social ants today; as far as is known, the truly solitary way of life disappeared long ago.

There is a tiny wasp *(Scleroderma macrogaster)* found in southern United States which is considered to be an ancestor of the ants, or at

This tiny wingless wasp (Scleroderma macrogaster) *is believed by some biologists to be an ancestor of the social ants. Its larva lives as a parasite in beetle grubs.*

least it evolved from the original ancestor of the ants. These small wasps are wingless and the female lays her eggs in beetle grubs where the young develop as internal parasites.

Ants of many kinds are still in the hunting stages of their evolution. Among the most primitive ants are Ponerine ants that live mostly by hunting. These ants are especially abundant in tropical countries where some of the world's most warlike ants occur. Among them are the savage bulldog ants *(Myrmecia)* of Australia and the vicious jumping ants *(Odontomachus* and *Harpegnathus)*. Other hunting ants are the large, black carpenter ants *(Camponotus)* so common here in our own country.

Ants of other kinds have arrived at the Pastoral Stage, these being the ants that keep livestock in the form of plant lice or aphids for the honeydew they secrete. A few ants, such as the fungus growers, have graduated up to the next rung in the ladder; these ants actually cultivate crops and feed upon them, so we can truthfully say that they have reached the Agricultural Stage. They, in a way, are the elite of the ant clans because this is as high as the ants have, so far, advanced. As a matter of fact, it is probable that this is as high as they will ever rise. It seems highly unlikely that ants, whose habits are governed by instinct, could ever develop societies engaged in commerce or industrial enterprises, and certainly not intellectual pursuits. But evolution often takes strange twists and perhaps, millions of years in the future, ants may develop social structures far beyond any they experience now. Who can say what the far distant future holds for either ants or men?

Chapter 2

The Ant World

ANTS ARE INSECTS of a special type; they make up a separate group. Like all insects, their bodies are covered with hard shells called exoskeletons. There are three body regions: *head,* mid-section or *thorax,* and *abdomen.* The head contains the eyes, antennae, mouth parts, and brain. To the thorax are attached the legs and, in the case of males and queens, the wings. The rear portion of the ant's body or abdomen contains several organs including most of the digestive system, the food-storage crop, the reproductive organs, and the sting, when it is present.

As in all insects, the shell-like body and legs of ants are jointed so as to allow movement. Such animals are classified as Arthropods, a term derived from two Greek words, *arthros* meaning "joint" and *podus* meaning "foot." All such animals have their skeletons on the outside and their organs on the inside. (In our bodies the reverse is true.) This hard, outer shell or exoskeleton has a number of advantages; it affords protection for the insect and enables muscles to work more efficiently. This is one of the reasons why ants appear to be very strong; their muscles, which are attached to the *insides* of their skeletons, have better leverage than our muscles. Some ants can lift more than fifty times their own weight.

An ant's digestive system is well fitted to the kind of life it leads. Like us, an ant has a stomach where food is stored during digestion, but just in front of the stomach is a crop or "storage stomach." This organ is very useful to ants since it can be used to carry or store liquid food which can later be regurgitated and fed to other adult ants or to their young. Bees have similar "storage stomachs" which they use as tanks for carrying nectar or honey. A valve prevents the contents of the "storage stomach" from passing on into the true stomach for di-

15

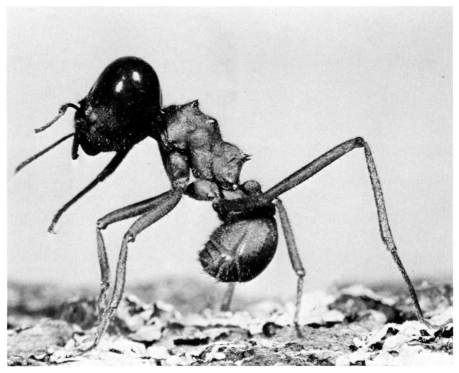

Ants' bodies are divided into three parts: the head, the thorax or mid-section, and the abdomen. Three pairs of legs are attached to the thorax. Like all insects, their bodies are encased in a hard, shell-like covering or exoskeleton and their legs are jointed. This is a leaf-cutting ant (Atta laevigata) *from Brazil.*

gestion and use by the individual insect. In some ants, such as honey ants, this "storage stomach" often becomes so distended by contained honey that it fills the entire abdomen and stretches it to enormous size. Ants are much more versatile than bees in their choice of foods; honeybees will eat only pollen and nectar, but most ants will eat whatever is available. However, they do have preferences; some ants are primarily carnivorous, others eat seeds, while still others eat sweets. If these foods are not obtainable, however, they will often turn to other foods. On the other hand, some ants are very specialized and will not change their food habits.

The nervous system of an ant is rather similar to our own but, instead of being located along the insect's back as in our bodies, it is located along the lower portion of its body. It consists of a brain located in the head and of a nerve cord along which are located enlarged

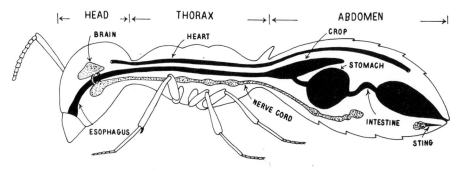

This diagram shows the internal structure of a typical ant: head, thorax, and abdomen. The tubular heart extends along the back from head to abdomen, and just below this is the digestive system. The crop is often used for storing food and this food can be regurgitated and fed to other ants or to their young. The nervous system consists of the brain located in the head and of a nerve cord running along the lower part of the body.

nerve centers or *ganglia* (singular, *ganglion*). Smaller nerves extend to all parts of the ant's body, including the various sense organs, legs, and wings.

An ant has a heart, but it differs considerably from our own; instead of being located in the "chest" cavity it consists of a hollow tube extending from the head to the rear portion of its body. This "heart" lies along the back just above the digestive system. Blood is caused to flow forward through this tubelike heart by a system of valves and muscular contractions. The blood empties into the head near the brain and then flows backward among the body organs.

It may seem remarkable indeed that all the above organs, and many more, can be contained within the tiny body of an ant. But all these necessary parts and organs are always present and are certainly an illustration of animal miniaturization. Consider also that the tiniest gnat you can see has, within its body, all these parts as well as hundreds of muscles enabling it to fly and walk about.

Since ants do not have the intelligence to make and use tools, they must rely upon those that Nature has given them. Their most useful "tools" are their jaws or mandibles which are often especially fitted to carry out various tasks. Some ants, such as carpenter ants, use their jaws to cut away solid wood. Harvester ants use their jaws to bite into flinty seeds, while leaf-cutting ants employ their sharp jaws to cut out

17

The ice-tong jaws of the Central American army ant (Eciton) soldier are fitted for fighting, not work.

Ants' jaws serve them in many ways. This is a close-up of the armed jaws of the Australian bulldog ant (Myrmecia), one of the world's most vicious hunters. It uses its jaws to capture game. Its vision is keen.

The sensitive "feelers" or antennae of ants must be kept free of dirt and dust. On the front legs of most ants is located a pair of combs through which the antennae can be drawn to remove dirt. This set of combs is from a Central American army ant (Eciton).

Hooked claws on the feet of almost all ants enable them to climb trees or walk on the undersides of leaves and limbs. These large claws are on the foot of an army ant (Eciton).

sections of leaves. Other ants use their jaws in digging, fighting, carrying young, and in numerous diverse ant activities. Many ants also use their legs to help them in various ways, in addition to their primary purpose of walking. Harvester ants, for example, dig with their feet like tiny dogs. Many ants have special, comblike or brushlike structures located on their front legs. These are used for cleaning the antennae. The ant lifts its leg and draws its antennae through the comb, brushing off any adhering dirt. Incidentally, all ants have the same number of segments or joints in their legs. These consist of two basal segments, the *coxa* and *trochanter*, a long *femur*, a slender *tibia*, and five *tarsal* or "foot" joints, the first of which may be longer than the others.

All animals are equipped to obtain information from the world about them. This is necessary in order that they may avoid enemies, hunt food, seek mates, build nests, and protect themselves from unfavorable climatic conditions. In general, ants have about the same sense organs that we have but they have, in addition, some that we do not have. Most ants have well-developed eyes and their vision is probably quite good, especially at close range. Like other insects, most of them have *compound* eyes; that is, their eyes are made up of a large number of tiny, individual eyes, each of which discerns a portion of the visual field. This is called *mosaic* vision and is especially effective in perceiving moving objects. While ants' eyes react to light in much the same way as our own, they apparently are red-blind. In other words, they cannot see in red light and red objects probably look black to them. For this reason, the habits of ants can be studied in red light under which they carry on their work just as though they were in darkness. There is another interesting difference in ants' eyes; they can detect polarized light, or light vibrating in only one plane. The sky is lighted with partly polarized light. This enables some ants to find their way over barren ground where they navigate by the sun's rays or by polarized sky light. Indeed, these ants have some sort of built-in timing mechanism that takes into consideration the hourly changes in the sun's angle. If a box is placed over an ant that has been crawling homeward across the sand, so that the ant is in the dark for an hour or so, it will start out again after the box is removed. However, its new direction of travel will not be the same as it was originally; it will be changed

Australian bulldog ants (Myrmecia) have well-developed eyes. These vicious ants live by hunting insects.

In the case of the army ants of Central America and the driver ants of Africa, only the winged males have eyes. Seen here is a close-up of the head of a male driver ant showing the three ocelli or simple eyes and the large compound eyes on the sides of its head.

to correspond to the new angle of the sun. Such an experiment shows that the ant is navigating by a built-in sun compass.

Some ants follow scent trails to places where food is abundant. The first ant that locates a good source of food returns to the nest but, as it walks along, it touches its abdomen to the ground, depositing tiny traces of scent. Other ants then follow this "blazed" trail out to the food. This is the reason why large numbers of ants soon gather around any bit of food such as a crust of bread discarded near a picnic. Ants, such as the harvesters (*Pogonomyrmex*), that gather seeds from prairie plants do not lay scent trails since such trails would usually be of little value. Seeds are scattered here and there on the ground and when a seed is found and carried back to the nest there is usually no reason for other ants to visit the same place. For this reason, harvester ants hunt by sight and navigate by landmarks, not by scent trails. Apparently, harvester ants learn their whole foraging area and can find their way home from any point within it. However, they do recognize and identify seeds by taste or smell. Unlike most other insects, ants seem to have considerable ability to learn.

Most ants have well-developed eyes, but some are completely blind. Shown here is a blind worker of the African driver ants. Only the large, winged males have eyes.

Soldier army ants (Eciton) *have very tiny eyes which are probably useless. They live in Central and South America.*

While King Solomon in the Bible stated that ants have no leaders or overseers to supervise their work, there do appear to be certain individuals in a colony who are always the first to begin work on a project. These have been called "work-starters" and perhaps are old, experienced veterans. Here we have individuals who may, in a sense, be regarded as leaders.

We normally assume that an animal that lives by hunting other creatures must be keen of vision, so it may come as a surprise to you to learn that the tropical army ants (*Eciton*) are blind. The same is true of African driver ants (*Dorylus*). Their foraging columns go through the jungle capturing and devouring other creatures, but they hunt by smell and follow scent trails. Apparently, their other senses serve them so well that they do not need eyes.

Smell and taste are closely related senses and ants can taste or detect odors with organs located on their legs and antennae as well as with their mouths. An ant's antennae are especially sensitive to odors and,

23

as can easily be noted by observing them, they use their antennae to investigate any possible food just as a dog uses its nose to sniff at a bone.

As far as hearing is concerned, ants have no "ears" as such. Grasshoppers have special eardrums or tympanic membranes for sound detection, but ants apparently hear sound vibrations from the surfaces upon which they are resting or, perhaps, through minute, sensitive hairs on their antennae. Some ants make sounds by rubbing one body part against another. In some ants, such as the leaf-cutters (*Atta*), there is a scraper on one abdominal segment that rubs against a file on another segment. This makes a squeeking sound that can be heard for several feet. Some of the large hunting ants (Ponerinae) have very large sound-making organs.

With regard to the living areas of ants, it would be very difficult to make a brief statement. They inhabit almost every bit of solid earth where the climate is warm enough. This extends from the southern tip of South America, New Zealand, and Australia to the Arctic Circle. They range from hot jungles to barren deserts and far up on our loftiest

This is one of the world's tiniest ants, photographed from a museum specimen. Known as Strumigenys, *these ants live in rotten wood where they form small colonies. Their food consists of springtails or collembola which they capture by stealth and patience. Their slender jaws can be opened until they almost touch the sides of their heads. After these jaws snap shut on a victim, it is stung to death.*

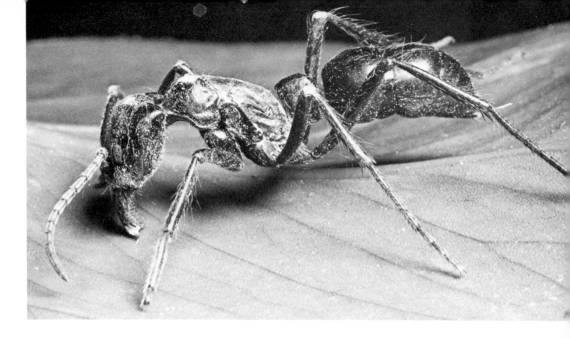

This is the largest ant in the world; individuals measure more than an inch in length. They live in holes in the ground in Brazil and their food consists of insects. They are known to science as Dinoponera grandis. BELOW: Another picture of Dinoponera grandis.

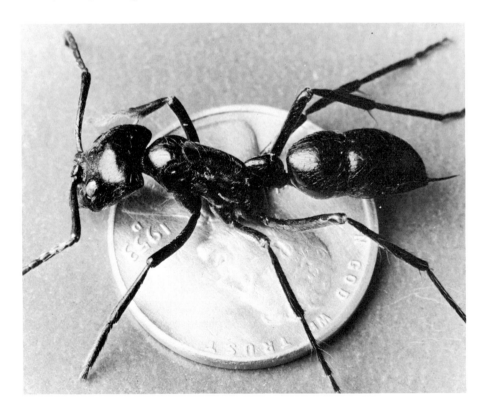

mountains, but tropical lands have more ants than cooler climates. It seems probable that ants were among the first insects to come to the notice of human beings. Their activities were recorded in the most ancient writings in Hebrew, Greek, Latin, and Chaldaic languages. Such writers as Pliny, Aristotle, Plutarch, Virgil, Hesiod, and Ovid all mention them.

Virgil (70 B.C.-19 B.C.), in his Aeneid, writes:

> Thus in battalia march embodied ants,
> Fearful of winter and of future wants,
> T'invade the corn, and to their cells convey,
> The plundered forage of their yellow prey.

In the above quotation, Virgil was no doubt speaking of the seed-harvesting ants (*Messor*). It definitely proves that the author knew something about the habits of these interesting ants.

Horace (65 B.C.-8 B.C.) also proves in verse that he was aware of the harvester ants. He says:

> The little ants, of great industry—that favorite
> model with the miser—bears away in her mandibles
> whatever she can, and adds it to the store which she is
> accumulating, nor unmindful nor improvident of the
> future.

One finds, in many writings of ancient authors, mention of these same ants which seem to have impressed people with their industry. Most everyone is familiar with the Biblical quotation from King Solomon in which he says, in part, "Go to the ant, thou sluggard; consider her ways and be wise: which having no guide, overseer, or ruler, provideth her meat in the summer, and gathereth her food in the harvest." (Proverbs VI: 6, 7, 8)

While ants are mentioned several times in the Bible, the ancient Biblical writers were conscious of other insects as well. Bees are mentioned four times, caterpillars and flies nine times each, grasshoppers and locusts thirty-four times, and worms twenty times.

Ants are mentioned also in ancient Hebrew writings. The Hebrew name for ant is *nemalah,* from the verb *namal,* to "cut off." This prob-

26

INSECT

UNSELFISHNESS
JUSTICE COURTESY

ANT

Ants are held in high regard in many lands. In Japan and China, the word for "ant" is made up of the character meaning "insect" and those meaning "unselfishness, justice, and courtesy."

ably refers to the cutting off of seeds by the harvester ants. The Arabic word for ant is similar; it is *nimala*.

From the above it is obvious that people have always been aware of ants and, in many instances, have used them as examples of integrity and industry. As evidence of the high regard in which ants are held, it might be mentioned that, in Japanese, the characters meaning "ant" also include those meaning "unselfishness, justice, and courtesy." While this is a pleasant designation and well intended, it may not be entirely deserved. Most ants are industrious, of course, but there are many kinds that enslave others, and yet other ants are vicious fighters. The tropical army ants and driver ants move through the forests like savage Mongol armies, killing and devouring every living creature in their paths. Other ants are thieves, making their living by stealing food from their industrious neighbors. Dr. W. M. Mann, former Director of the National Zoological Park in Washington, D. C., once noticed, in Arizona, that there were great numbers of large ant heads near a harvester ant nest. These were the heads of the miller caste, big-headed ants that cut up flinty seeds for the rest of the colony. When the seed-harvesting season was over, the millers had been beheaded and tossed out since their work for the year was ended and their presence during the winter would be a useless drain on the colony's economy. These ants are close relatives to the ants which King Solomon observed in the Holy Land and considered to be so virtuous! Still, we cannot condemn all ants

27

Harvester ants (Pogonomyrmex) *feed upon flinty seeds. Here is a "portrait" of a harvester ant soldier or "miller" that uses its short, powerful jaws to cut seeds.*

merely because some kinds seem, in our eyes, to have strayed from the paths of righteousness.

In the world, there are more than 8,000 different kinds or species of ants. Many of these occur in our climate but, in the Tropics, ants reach their greatest abundance and diversity in both habits and size. In many tropical lands ants are so important as agricultural pests that they literally control the economy of the countries. This is especially true of the leaf-cutting ants *(Atta)* of Central and South America. Here in our own country there are ants of several kinds that infest homes, and others that are serious agricultural pests. One of these is the imported fire ant *(Solenopsis saevissima richteri)* which was first discovered near Mobile, Alabama, having entered this country as a stowaway on a ship from South America. This viciously stinging ant has now spread to many southeastern states where large sums are being spent in efforts to eradicate it. This ant lives in the ground, constructing high mounds or "hills." Some people are especially sensitive to their venom and have required hospitalization after being stung. Research carried on by the writer has shown that fish are often killed by eating fire ants which have fallen into the water.

On the Great Plains of North America the large mounds of the harvester ants are characteristic features of the landscape. These mounds may be a foot or more in height and the spaces surrounding them are usually cleared of all vegetation. In view of their seed-collecting habits and the fact that they clear the areas around their nests, thus destroying the vegetation, they are considered to be agricultural pests on rangelands.

Regardless of where we go we usually encounter ants of one kind

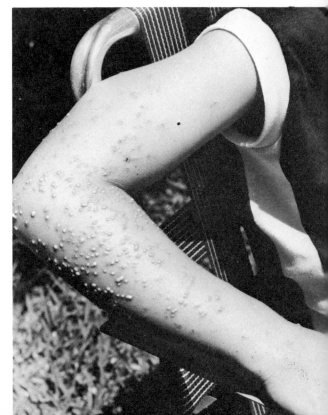

Some people are especially sensitive to ant stings. Shown here is a small boy's arm which had received numerous stings by imported fire ants.

or another. No picnic is complete without ants! They vary in size from tiny thief ants *(Solenopsis molesta),* common here in the United States, to the great *tucandero* ant of Brazil which measures more than an inch in length.

Not only do ants vary in size of the individuals but in colony size as well. Many kinds have very small colonies, often only a dozen or so. On the other hand, some ant colonies are very large; a red ant colony *(Formica)* was found to contain 238,000 individuals, while a colony of migratory army ants *(Eciton)* may have a million individuals.

As a general rule, ants are not colorful; most of them are black, brown, or rust color. Yet in the Tropics, the "ant capital" of the world, are found a few very pretty ants. One example is the *Macromischa* ant of the West Indies that is colored in beautiful hues of metallic green, purple, and red. Another colorful ant is the tailor ant *(Oecophylla)* of the East Indies and other areas of the Old World Tropics. Some kinds of these ants are green, while others are red. One kind found in Africa is black, in keeping with the name of the Dark Continent. Even here in our own country are found a few ants with metallic coloration. Among these are *Pheidole metalescens,* found from North Carolina westward to Texas and on into Mexico.

The life histories of ants are said to be "complete"; that is, they pass through four stages or steps during their development. Eggs, laid by the queen, hatch into tiny, grublike larvae. These larval ants are blind and legless and usually smallest at the front end. During this helpless stage they are fed and cared for by adult worker ants or nurses. As seasons and temperatures vary, these young are moved about in the nest and placed in cells or chambers where conditions are most ideal for their growth. During this stage they are fed on food regurgitated from the mouths of the nurses. This food, of course, depends upon the food habits of the ants. In the case of hunting ants, the food consists of masticated bits of captured insects, while in the case of ants that feed upon vegetable material, the food is mostly vegetable in nature. Honey ants, that gather and store honeydew, feed their larvae on this honey-like material. Ants of other kinds cultivate fungi and it is upon fungus food that their young are fed.

When fully developed, the larval ants transform into *pupae.* These

Here we see an acrobatic ant (Crematogaster) *collecting honeydew from a plant. It will be stored in the ant's crop for transportation back to the nest.*

pupal ants are helpless and do not feed. When examined under a hand lens it can be seen that all the external parts of the future ants are visible, but they are white and waxlike. Some ant pupae are enclosed in parchment-like cocoons which the larvae spin before transforming into the pupal stage, while other pupae are naked. The cocoons are oval in shape and usually white, though a few, such as those of the honey ants, are gray. When an ant nest is broken open in summer, large numbers of these cocoons can be seen and it is actually these that many people call ant "eggs." Ant eggs are very tiny and difficult to see except through a lens.

The time required for the growth of an ant varies with the kind, but the development of the red ant may be taken as an average example. In these ants, it has been found that the egg stage lasts about 24 days, the larval stage from 30 to 71 days, and the pupal stage about 20 days. From this it is apparent that about three months pass from the time eggs are laid until the adult stage is reached.

One of the most unusual things about ants is the fact that, in some

31

The jaws of leaf-cutting ants (Atta) are well fitted for cutting sections out of leaves, which they carry into their nests and use as a compost upon which to cultivate a special fungus. This one is from Panama.

kinds, not all individuals in a nest are alike. This is called *polymorphism*, a term meaning that their body forms are of many kinds. In a colony of leaf-cutting ants *(Atta)*, for example, there are workers of several sizes, among which there is a rather definite division of labor. Each size is fitted to the type of work it does. Not only are there variations in size, but there are often differences in eyes, antennae, mandibles, and other parts. Indeed, some authorities consider that there are nearly thirty kinds or forms of ants, many of which have been given special names. Unusually large workers are called *macrogates*; dwarf workers are called *microgates*. Individuals having the size and form of the worker combined with the thorax of a queen are called *pseudo-*

gynes. In the case of western honey ants, certain individual workers take on the duty of serving as storage tanks for honeydew, with the result that their abdomens become greatly swollen. These individuals are known as *repletes.* In some ants, such as the harvesters *(Pogono-myrmex),* there is a soldier caste and these individuals are called *diner-gates.* These ants have large heads and jaws and their duties consist of crushing seeds or defending the nest. In the case of the trap-door ants *(Colobopsis)* which live inside twigs, the soldiers have plug-shaped heads which are used as living doors to close the entrances to their tunnels. Soldiers appear to have different duties in different ants.

All the above ants—that is, the workers and soldiers—are imperfect or undeveloped females that never have wings and do not mate and lay eggs. They arise from fertilized eggs. We have already seen that, in addition to these, there are egg-laying queens and male ants, both of which usually have wings. Male ants, like drone honeybees, result from unfertilized eggs. After mating, the queen severs her wings and from that time on is wingless like her workers.

As a general rule, worker ants live for only a few months or perhaps

The workers of many ants have stings like bees. This is the greatly enlarged sting of the Australian bulldog ant (Myrmecia) *which can inflict a painful sting.*

a year but some workers may survive to a ripe old age of five or six years. On the other hand, there are records of captive queens that have lived much longer. A queen of a European ant *(Lasius aliens)* lived for ten years, while a queen of another European ant *(Formica fusca)* lived in an artificial nest from December, 1874, to August, 1888. Since the age of this queen was unknown when captured it seems probable that she lived for at least fifteen years. This queen was kept by Sir John Lubbock, the noted ant authority of England, and she established a record for longevity that will probably stand for a long while.

It may be helpful in our discussions of ants if we know something about the way in which they are classified. The ant family FORMICIDAE is divided into six subfamilies as follows:

Subfamily DORYLINAE: from the Greek word for "spear," in reference to their stings. In many ways these are the most interesting and remarkable of all ants. Most of them are native to tropical lands but some kinds occur in the United States. Their eyes are either very small or absent, and the queens and workers are wingless; only the males have wings. Pupae are either enclosed in cocoons or naked, depending on the species. These ants live by hunting other insects or, sometimes, larger prey, even domestic animals, which they will often attack regardless of size. They have no permanent nests, but move from place to place in large armies. From time to time they settle down to rear young, then move on again, hunting as they go. These are the famous army ants *(Eciton)* of the American Tropics and the driver ants *(Dorylus)* of Africa. *Eciton* ants are also found in North America but they are smaller in size than their cousins in the Tropics.

Subfamily PONERINAE: from the Greek meaning "bad" or "painful," because of their fierceness. These ants vary in size from very tiny to about an inch in length. Many kinds dwell in the Tropics where they feed upon other insects. Usually their nests are in the ground and consist of only a few individuals, usually less than thirty. They are primitive hunters, and many kinds sting severely. Their pupae spin cocoons.

In these primitive ants the caste system is but poorly developed. In some *(Leptogenys)* there are no winged queens, the eggs being laid by an egg-laying worker if the queen is killed. In the case of bulldog ants *(Myrmecia)* the mated queens seem in no hurry to found their colonies.

34

Subfamily Dolichoderinae: On top of the tree limb is shown Tapinoma, *a common ant. Some kinds live in the Tropics where they nest in trees or in air plants. Beneath the tree limb is shown an Argentine ant* (Iridomyrmex), *a South American ant now found in southern United States.*

Subfamily Dorylinae: At lower left is the African driver ant (Dorylus), *the one shown being a soldier. At lower right is the army ant* (Eciton) *of Central America, this one also a soldier. The workers of both kinds are smaller than the soldiers and have smaller jaws.*

Subfamily Leptaleinae: The slender ant (Pseudomyrma) *shown at the top lives within the hollow thorns of the bull-horn acacia in Central and South America. This small tree produces many of these hornlike thorns. Note the ant entrance holes in one of each pair of thorns.*

Subfamily Ponerinae: At the left is the kelep ant (Ectatomma) *of Central America. This ant was once introduced into Texas to destroy the cotton boll weevil. At the lower right is the mata ant* (Dinoponera gigantea) *of Brazil which is more than an inch in length and stings severely.*

They may live alone in small burrows for several months but when they do excavate a nest and lay eggs they leave the entrance open. While the young are growing the queen makes expeditions into the surrounding area to capture game. Some Ponerine ants fight among themselves for food and may even practice cannibalism at times. In other words, among these primitive ants, the true spirit of community cooperation is not yet fully developed. Their "civilizations" correspond, perhaps, to those of ancient cave-dwelling humans.

Among the ants belonging to this subfamily are the Australian bulldog ants *(Myrmecia gulosa)*, the hunting ants *(Ponera)*, and the jumping ants *(Myrmecia nigrocincta)* of Australia.

Subfamily LEPTALEINAE: from a Greek word meaning "slender." This is the smallest subfamily since it contains only a few kinds of species. Within the United States there is but one kind, the small *Leptalea* ants which nest in the stems of grasses and in branches of trees. Most interesting of all are the *Pseudomyrma* ants which live within the hollow thorns of bull-horn acacias in Mexico and Central America. They sting viciously.

Subfamily Myrmecinae: In this large group are included ants having various habits. At the upper left is seen a winged queen of Aphaenogaster, *a native of the Tropics. At upper right is the common acrobatic ant* (Crematogaster). *At center, left, is the fire ant* (Solenopsis) *found in southern United States. The ant carrying a seed at lower left is one of the harvester ants* (Pheidole), *and at lower right is the leaf-cutting ant* (Atta).

Subfamily Formicinae: This is a large group whose members vary widely in habits. At upper left is the trap-door ant (Colobopsis). On the tree facing downward is the carpenter ant (Camponotus) which excavates its nest in wood. On the leaves is a tailor ant (Oecophylla) which uses its larvae as a source of silk to sew leaves together. It is found in the East Indies. Just to the right of the tree is the slave-making ant (Polyergus). At extreme right is the common red mound-building ant (Formica). Beneath the ground is the honey ant (Myrmecocystus) of our Southwest which uses its abdomen as a storage tank for honeydew.

Subfamily MYRMICINAE: from the Greek word meaning "ant." This is the largest group of ants and they are found almost everywhere. Among them are many common kinds. They are typical "ants," usually having eyes and with their pupae naked. The workers may have stings. As a general rule, these ants feed mostly upon vegetable material and some kinds cultivate fungus gardens. Others feed upon honeydew obtained from aphids and other insects. Still others are pests in homes and gardens. Included here are such ants as the harvesters *(Pogonomyrmex)* which gather seeds, the leaf-cutting or parasol ants *(Atta)* which cultivate fungi, the acrobatic ants *(Crematogaster)*, King Solomon's ant *(Messor)*, and the fire ants *(Solenopsis)*.

Subfamily DOLICHODERINAE: from Greek, meaning "long neck." These are small ants, many kinds of which have characteristic odors. They have no stings and their abdomens are oval with no "waist" between the first and second segments. Their pupae do not spin cocoons.

These ants often walk about with their abdomens bent over their backs and they are common almost everywhere. Often they are found associated with aphids or plant lice and other honeydew-secreting insects. Some common examples include the Argentine ant *(Iridomyrmex humilis)* found in our country, the erratic ant *(Tapinoma erraticum)* of Europe which squirts an offensive fluid on enemies, and the odorous house ant *(Tapinoma sessile)* found in the United States.

FORMICINAE: from the Latin *formica* meaning "ant." These are typical ants and to this subfamily belong the majority of all common kinds. They vary in size from very tiny to nearly an inch in length and have heavy, toothed jaws. Their habits are varied and, while they are found almost everywhere, they are especially numerous in tropical lands. They have no stings and there is no constriction or "waistline" between the first and second segments of the abdomen. Their pupae are usually enclosed in cocoons. Some common examples are: carpenter ants *(Camponotus)*, the slave-making ants *(Formica)*, the brown ants *(Lasius)*, the Australian honey ants *(Meloporus)*, the American honey ants *(Myrmecocystus)*, the robber ants *(Polyergus)*, and the tropical tailor ants *(Oecophylla)*.

Chapter 3

The Hunters

As we have seen, the ant realm is divided into six tribes or subfamilies. The first two, the Dorylinae and Ponerinae, are the most primitive and it is among the ants belonging to these two groups that are found the most important hunting ants. The Mongols of the ant kingdom are the Doryline or warrior ants so common in many tropical lands. Their story is recounted in a later chapter. While the warrior ants are the world's most outstanding hunting insects, many of the Ponerine ants, too, have reputations as enthusiastic hunters of game.

Ponerine colonies are usually small and they favor underground nests. As far as social habits are concerned, they are quite primitive; their queens do not have retinues of workers to feed and care for them and neither are they the only egg-laying females in the colony. In some cases, the queen as such cannot be distinguished from her sisters and, in others, if the queen dies, the duty of laying eggs is taken over by a worker. In only rare cases are soldiers present. Even in their mating habits, the queens make little show of their royal lineage. In the case of the Ponerine ants found in North America, both males and queens are winged but only the males actually take to the air. There is no mating or nuptial flight; the queens remain near the nest entrances where they are visited by flying males. After mating, the queen is still not ready to found a new colony. She plays it safe; her first workers are reared in the family nest. Actually, this is much easier than starting a colony by herself as do the queens of most other ants. After her first young have transformed into adult workers she takes off out into the unknown with a number of them and establishes a new colony. In this respect, the habits of these queens are like those of the queen honeybee who swarms out of the parent colony with a group of workers.

This strange ant (Daceton) *is found in the Tropics where it captures and feeds* *upon insects. It is closely related to* Strumigenys, *one of the world's smallest* *ants. Here are two views of it.*

While the above procedure is followed by the queens of some North American Ponerine ants *(Stigmatomma* and *Ponera)*, others start colonies by themselves. Among the more interesting of these hunting ants are the bulldog ants *(Myrmecia)* of Australia and other places. These ants are of large size, in some cases almost an inch long, and often conspicuously colored in shades of red. They have large eyes and jaws as befit those who live by the hunt. Their tunnels extend deeply into the earth, sometimes to depths of four or more feet. They are the tigers of the ant world; it is said that the workers of one kind "will follow an intruder for quite thirty feet from the nest in the hope of getting a parting bite." Ian R. Bock of the University of Queensland, Australia, has had considerable experience with these remarkable ants near his home. He states that "they are particularly aggressive and vicious; when the nest is disturbed, large numbers run towards the cause of the disturbance and march across the leaf litter with a sound like gentle rain. Their stings are very painful." This *Myrmecia (M. forficata)* is nocturnal in its habits; that is, it hunts by night. Another kind *(M. nigrocincta)* found in Australia has been called "jumper" ants because of their habit of jumping out of the nest entrances like packs of tiny dogs ready to attack an intruder. Still another bulldog ant *(M. gulosa)* of Australia often attacks and kills large beetles, and some kinds can jump a foot or more. They are also swimmers and do not hesitate to enter water.

The habits of some *Myrmecia* queens are quite unusual. Before settling down to establish colonies, they may roam about for months, stopping now and then to dig small burrows and to feed. Having at last "decided" that it is time to settle down and cease her wanderings, the queen excavates a tunnel and lays a few eggs, but she does not seal the outside entrance as do most other queens. Now and then she goes hunting and brings fresh "meat" home to her young. These young, like some other ant larvae, have convenient, troughlike cavities on their abdomens which serve as "dishes" for their food. In the case of *Stigmatomma*, one of our native Ponerine ants, food is simply tossed to the larvae who fight over it like small dogs.

Among these savage ants, there is little of the cooperation between sister ants so common among ants of other kinds. The workers do not exchange food; each one hunts on its own. Strangely, the various kinds

41

The Australian bulldog ants (Myrmecia) are among the world's most vicious hunters. An inch long, they have long jaws armed with teeth. They are alert and aggressive and have excellent eyesight. In Australia, they are found near the coastal areas. The ones shown here are Myrmecia gulosa.

Here is an Australian bulldog ant of another kind (Myrmecia forceps). *It is common in eucalyptus forests of Australia.*

The nests of bulldog ants are abundant in the open eucalyptus forests of Australia. Here is shown (arrow) the entrance to one such ant nest near Brisbane, Australia.

I. R. BOCK,
UNIVERSITY OF QUEENSLAND

Australian bulldog ants nest in the ground. If the nest is disturbed the ants come bouncing out of their holes like tiny wolves bent on attack. Since they can bite and sting, their attacks are not to be taken lightly. Some kinds will follow an intruder for several yards.

This is Odontomachus, one of the world's most unusual ants. Slender in body form like a greyhound, it can open its jaws very wide. It moves along the ground until it encounters a pebble, insect, or other object. Its open jaws are then snapped shut upon the object with such force that the ant is thrown through the air. Almost an inch in length, these are among the world's most ferocious ants. This one lived in the Solomon Islands.

These "portraits" of Odontomachus *show its slender, toothed jaws that it can open very wide. These ants feed upon insect game and are sometimes called "tic-ants." Some kinds are found in southern United States.*

of Ponerine ants tend to specialize in their prey; one kind in Australia captures and devours queen ants, one in South Africa is partial to beetles, a South American variety eats termites, and one kind found in Texas feeds entirely on sowbugs. Dr. C. D. Michener, well-known authority on social insects, states that other American Ponerine ants (*Stigmatomma* and *Ponera*) feed on millipedes which are usually found in damp situations. In general, the food of most of these hunting ants consists of termites which are an ideal "game" animal since they are defenseless and usually abundant. In fact, it seems probable that the chief duty of termite soldiers is the protection of their colonies from Ponerine ants which are ancient termite enemies.

It is said that in the case of a large South African hunting ant (*Megaponera foetens*), termite colonies are hunted by scout workers. When a likely colony is located the scout guides her sisters to the site and the termite nest is plundered and the helpless inmates carried home in the jaws of their captors. While going about their murderous business, the large ants make sounds loud enough to be heard by human

The imported fire ant is a native of South America but now occurs in our South-east. It builds large earthen mounds and feeds mostly upon insects. It stings severely.

ears. These sounds are given either as battle cries or to coordinate the attack on the termites.

Hunting ants of several kinds have developed the ability to jump. In addition to the *Myrmecias* mentioned previously, this grasshopper-like characteristic is found among such hunting ants as *Harpegnathus* and *Odontomachus*. The latter ants occur in southern Florida, Texas, and Arizona as well as many tropical areas. Our largest hunting ants, the largest ant of any kind in North America, is *Neoponera villosa* which ranges all the way from southern Texas southward to Brazil. These ants are about one-half inch in length and run rapidly over the ground. They sting severely and feed upon insects.

While the primitive Ponerine ants are almost all hunters, there are many other kinds of ants that also prey on small creatures. Even the harvester ants *(Pogonomyrmex)* which normally store and eat seeds, will often devour other insects. The fire ants *(Solenopsis)* feed upon both seeds and insects. The imported fire ant *(Solenopsis saevissima richteri)* apparently feeds on small insects but it also gathers sweet honeydew from aphids or plant lice. In its native home in South America these ants are considered to be more or less beneficial because of their food habits. In southeastern United States, however, where these ants now occur, they are serious pests because of their large mounds and stinging habits.

Ants in general may be considered beneficial to us because many of them feed upon various insects, some of which are pests. A large ant colony may destroy large numbers of insects. One myrmecologist (a student of ants) observed a colony of hunting ants and noted that they brought in twenty-eight dead insects per minute. At this rate, he estimated that 10,000 insects were consumed each day during their hours of greatest activity. As an indication of the high regard in which the red wood ant *(Formica rufa)* has been held in Europe, it might be mentioned that a German law passed in 1880 imposed a fine of 100 marks on anyone known to disturb a nest.

Among the most bloodthirsty of our native hunting ants are

Like many other ants, the imported fire ants follow scent paths to and from food sources. As they walk along, they mark their trails with a chemical substance.

the carpenter ants *(Camponotus)*. There are several different kinds but they are all of large size and usually live in tunnels which they chisel in wood with their powerful jaws. This habit, of course, is the origin of their name. Probably our best known kind is the black carpenter ant *(C. herculeanus pennsylvanicus)* which excavates its tunnels in decaying trees or telephone poles. In some cases it also injures the timbers of human habitations. These ants are about one-third of an inch long and can bite severely if carelessly handled. Usually, however, they are satisfied to escape, if this is possible. The workers hunt individually and can often be seen walking about among fallen leaves on the forest floor. Captured game, which may be any small creature

Formica ants are hunters of game which they capture by lone combat. Here is a red Formica *tugging at the antenna of a large bug it has killed.*

This is another Australian bulldog ant (Myrmecia brevinoda) *that is found near Brisbane.*

such as an insect, is carried back to the nest. How far from the nest they forage is unknown, but it is believed to be usually less than a hundred feet.

I once placed some of these ants in an artificial nest which I had built by setting two panes of glass in a wooden frame. The next morning all the inmates were gone, having cut a hole through the wood. Foolishly, I had forgotten that I was dealing with ants well equipped to cut through solid wood. Having learned this lesson, I then placed a colony, including their large queen, in an all-glass container and fed them on pieces of meat. They established themselves within a piece of rotten wood I had provided and began rearing young. When meat was placed in the glass container near their den they emerged like tiny, black wolves and tore off pieces with their jaws. When the feeding ants were watched under a lens, the sight was almost frightening. I could not help but be thankful that they were not the size of tigers! The realm of the hunting ants is truly a miniature world of violence and bloodshed where no quarter is asked and none is ever given.

Chapter 4

The Warrior Ants

MOST SPECTACULAR of all the world's ants and, in many ways, the most remarkable are the legionary or warrior ants of tropical forests. These ants, of which there are several kinds, all belong to the subfamily Dorylinae. The chief ones in Africa, known as driver ants, belong to the genus *Dorylus*, while the army ants of the American Tropics are classified in the genus *Eciton*. The most important and well known of these latter ants is *Eciton hamatum* which ranges over a wide area of tropical America. Closely related ants are found in our Southeast but their habits are not nearly as spectacular as are those of their cousins of the Tropics. One of our southern species is *Eciton schmitti*, found from Texas eastward to the Carolinas and northward to Kansas. These ants, like their tropical relatives, are nomadic, moving from place to place and occupying temporary nests. Like Mongol tribes, they live by plundering. They invade the nests of other ants to destroy and carry off their young. Sometimes they also capture adult ants and raid termite nests.

All the warrior ants are hunters first, last, and always. Their columns stream through the tropical forests killing and devouring anything small enough for them to attack. The African driver ants, as we shall see, may even attack large animals. Strangest of all, is the fact that these ants are blind! Only the large wasplike, winged males have eyes. It would seem that keen vision would be a necessity to insects which live by the hunt but, apparently, other senses serve them well so they have no need for eyes. Still, we cannot help but wonder why their eyes have disappeared. Once, probably several million years ago, their ancestors did have eyes. Evidence of this is found in several kinds of warrior ants in which the workers have tiny eyes which apparently serve no pur-

Portrait of a soldier. This driver ant with its sharp jaws can bite severely. It will attack almost any animal. Since it is blind, it probably does not know how large its enemy is.

This is the two-inch, winged male driver ant. Wasplike in appearance, these males have well-developed eyes. The queen is even larger than the male but, like the soldiers and workers, is blind.

Here a soldier driver ant is shown with a winged male. Note the difference in size.

A soldier driver ant (left) is shown with a small-sized worker for comparison. Some workers are even smaller than this. Except for the winged males, all driver ants are completely blind; they do not even have simple, useless eyes as do the army ants of the American Tropics.

pose. Such tiny, useless eyes are found in the *Eciton* ants, but the African *Dorylus* or driver ants lack even these.

Another interesting thing about these ants is the fact that the workers are *polymorphic*; that is, they are of various sizes. They vary from about three-sixteenths of an inch to three-eighths of an inch and have relatively small jaws. The soldiers, by contrast, have very long, curved jaws and measure nearly a half-inch in length. The queen has an elongate body and is considerably larger than the soldiers. In the case of the African driver ants, the queen is truly enormous; she is about two inches long. Army ant workers are equipped with stings.

One of the first naturalists to observe and write about the army ants was Henry Walter Bates, who said of them in 1892:

> "Wherever they pass, all the rest of the animal world is thrown into a state of alarm. They stream along the ground and climb to the summit of all the lower trees searching every leaf to its apex. Where booty is plentiful, they concentrate all their forces upon it, the dense phalanx of shining and quickly moving bodies, as it spreads over the surface, looking like a flood of dark-red liquid. All soft-bodied and inactive insects fall an easy prey to them, and they tear their victims in pieces for facility in carriage. Then, gathering together again in marching order, onward they move, the margins of the phalanx spread out at times like a cloud of skirmishers from the flanks of an army."

No better description could be given of the raiding marches of these remarkable ants which live in colonies consisting of, perhaps, a million individuals.

Most of the scientific information we have regarding the lives of the American army ants *(Eciton)* has been obtained from studies made on Barro Colorado Island in the Panama Canal Zone. Here on this island in Gatun Lake is located a research station where biologists may go to study plants and animals in primitive, tropical surroundings. Excellent laboratories and living facilities are available to visiting scientists. The island is relatively small, consisting of nearly 4,000 acres of forested land through which extend many trails. The forest is of the jungle or rain forest type having very heavy rainfall, especially during the

54

When photographed against a white background, this army ant soldier seems not to be hairy. Even though these ants have tiny eyes, they are considered to be blind. They use their sensitive antennae instead of eyes. (See next photograph)

When this same ant was photographed against a black background, the hairs covering its body are readily evident. Even its sickle-like jaws are hairy.

months from May through December. The dry season extends from January through April, which is the best time to study the army ants in their native habitat. Studies during the wet season are difficult since both temperature and humidity are too high for human comfort.

On Barro Colorado Island are found army ants of several kinds, but our discussion here will be confined to *Eciton hamatum* since it is probably the most interesting and typical. The behavior of these ants has been studied in detail by Dr. T. C. Schneirla of the American Museum of Natural History.

These ants march through the jungle in columns, usually about five ants wide. The rate of march is usually a little over a hundred feet an hour, which is quite fast considering their small size. As they move along over the floor of the forest, the front of the ant army fans out. If game is discovered they rush to the attack and tear it to bits which are carried back to the bivouac area. In the meantime, the rest of the ants re-form their columns and move on again. Their progress through the forests has been well described by comparing it to water flowing across the ground. Blindly they hurry on, their sensitive antennae bent forward.

Army ant soldiers with large jaws and the workers travel in columns through tropical forests. They capture insects and other small creatures which are cut up and carried back to the camping area. They build no permanent nests.

Not always, however, are these marching ant columns bent on raids; sometimes they are in the process of emigrating or moving to new quarters. If all the ants are traveling in one direction, one can be fairly sure that they are moving to a new area, but if groups are traveling in opposite directions it is probable that they are on raiding expeditions. Generally speaking, these army ants plunder the nests of other kinds of ants both for their young and adults. They also prey on wasp nests, scorpions, cockroaches, and any other insects available. They also capture spiders. If the ants are on a raiding safari there is usually not much evidence of the sickle-jawed soldiers standing guard along the line of march, but if they are emigrating to a new area, accompanied by their large queen, soldiers are stationed along the edges of the columns. The raids usually begin at dawn and may last all morning. Within the column can be seen workers carrying booty back to the nest. This is always carried beneath the ants' bodies as they hurry along. Sometimes, if game is too long for one ant to carry, they team up, with several ants straddling it and transporting it along. This may occur in the case of a caterpillar, for example. Sometimes the smaller workers ride along on booty being carried by their larger sisters. But, in general, the raiding columns seem to travel in a hit-or-miss fashion since there is no apparent evidence of leadership.

Like the native humans who live in the Tropics, the army ants indulge in a mid-day siesta; between 11:00 A.M. and 2:00 P.M. their activity slows down. Again in the afternoon their raiding columns may leave the nests and fan out through the forest in search of food to nourish the enormous colony of voracious ants and their young.

Army ants build no permanent nests and have no fixed homes but move around like gypsies; they are nomadic wanderers and only pause now and again during their travels to rear young. Periodically, they move on again as if driven by some deep-seated urge to seek new territory. The distance they travel to new bivouacs or campsites varies considerably; often the new site may be as far as a thousand feet from the former one. This, of course, has a practical explanation; if these large colonies of hunting ants were to remain in one place, the local "game" would soon be all consumed. Those who live by the hunt must be continually on the move. But there is more to the migrations of these

The duty of the big-jawed soldiers is the defense of the colony. Their jaws are not fitted for other work. Here are shown two soldiers and a worker (center) carrying a pincer from a captured scorpion.

Here we see a close-up of the worker carrying the scorpion pincer. Army ants can carry heavy weights.

strange ants than mere search for new hunting areas; their migratory movements are timed exactly with the reproductive cycle of the queen. For seventeen days they are on the move, stopping each night to form a cluster in some sheltered location. Here they cling together in a large mass, forming a living ball of ants. Deep within this cluster is the queen. Actually, the clusters are living nests, since the ants lock themselves together in a tight mass, leaving passages inside where the young and the queen can crawl about. By the end of the seventeen-day period of wandering from place to place, the larvae which were hatched from eggs laid during the last stationary period have changed into the pupal stage and are in their cocoons. The colony now settles down in some sheltered location and begins a period of settled life which lasts about twenty days during which daily hunting safaris are made into the surrounding jungle and booty is carried back to the nest.

The queen, already many times larger than her workers, now begins to fill with developing eggs. Her abdomen may swell to more than five times normal size. When her eggs are fully developed she begins laying them, often at the rate of nearly a hundred per hour, and within a week may lay more than 30,000. During this period, hunting raids are reduced, since there is not much activity and less food is needed. Eventually, after about two weeks, the enormous number of eggs laid by the queen begins hatching and all these larvae require food. In the meantime, the cocoons carried along from the previous stationary (sometimes called *statary*) camp have hatched and these young adults (called *callow* ants) also require food. Thus, with many new mouths to feed, the daily hunting raids increase in scope. At first, the callow workers are pale in color and do not take part in raids, but within about five days they gradually become darker and enter into all the activities of the colony.

Once more the ants set out on their wanderings, leaving each bivouac area in the evening, usually between 3:00 and 6:00 P.M. and traveling until about 9:00 P.M. The larvae are carried along by the workers. For the next seventeen days the ants move from place to place, traveling at night and raiding by day, but during the last nomadic day they carry the larvae out of the nesting area and allow them to spin cocoons. The colony now settles down in one place again for

Army ants form nest clusters by interlocking their bodies together to protect the queen and the young. African driver ants also use this technique to cross streams.

about twenty days. Thus, the nomadic periods alternate with the stationary or statary periods. This goes on forever; it is the way of life of the army ants.

The production of new colonies of these remarkable ants resembles, in a general way, the production of new swarms by a colony of honeybees. At certain seasons, the ants produce males and females, but only the males have wings. Having wings, these males may fly away to mate with new queens from other colonies. Only about half a dozen queens are produced and, after mating, one of these apparently becomes the "favorite." This queen then goes off with about half the colony, leaving the rest with the old queen. Thus does a new colony of army ants come into being.

Cycle of the army ants' lives. For about seventeen days they move to new campsites each night, carrying their larvae along. By the end of this period the larvae are ready to spin cocoons. For the next twenty days the colony remains in one place while the queen lays eggs. Daily raids are made to capture game. When the eggs hatch, the ants take to the road once more.

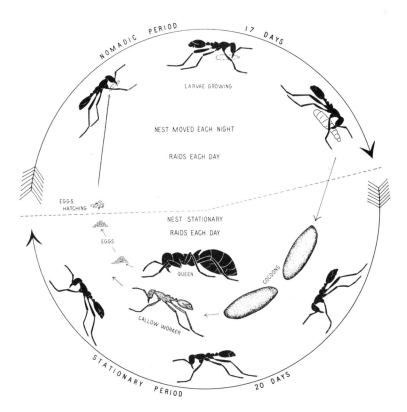

Growing larvae of army ants are carried from one campsite to another each night. When the larvae are fully developed, a stationary camp is established where they spin their cocoons. Shortly, the large, wingless queen begins laying eggs and when these hatch, the army begins traveling again.

A worker (left) and a soldier (right). Note the great difference in the size of their jaws. Workers are of several sizes.

The raids of the army ants are always most fascinating to watch. As the columns of ants hurry down their pathways they are accompanied by camp followers of many kinds; there are various insects, including small beetles as well as mites, which run along with the ants and which share in the kills. Some of these *myrmecophiles* or "ant lovers" are so lazy that they actually ride on the backs of the ants. Also accompanying the ants on their raids may be ant birds and flies, all bent on sharing in the spoils of battle. Probably the most interesting of these camp followers are the flies which hover over, or just ahead of, the raiding columns. These flies are not interested in the game killed by the ants but in the cockroaches and crickets which are flushed out of the leaves and vegetation through which the ants pass. When one of these insects is flushed and attempts to escape from the ants, one of these flies is apt to dart at it, depositing an egg or a living larva upon it. The larval flies then develop as parasites within the bodies of the roaches or crickets as the case may be. Some kinds of these flies deposit eggs while others deposit larvae. The flies could, of course, parasitize the roaches and crickets without the presence of the ants, but the ants certainly make it easier for them to see their prey. These

Another view of an army ant (Eciton) *soldier. This one lived in the mountains of Panama.*

The black army ant (Labidus) ranges through Central and South America where it lives by raiding the nests of other ants and devouring them. This one lived in Paraguay. It, too, is blind.

flies usually appear over the columns of ants within ten minutes after the start of a raid, attracted, probably, by the odor of the ants. On the average, about sixty flies will be found buzzing over the moving ant columns or alighting upon nearby weeds and bushes awaiting the emergence of prey from hiding places. It is often possible to locate the columns of army ants by the loud buzzing of the flies, which belong to two families: the thick-headed flies or Conopidae, and the parasitic flies or Tachinidae. The most usual ones involved are *Calodixia, Androeuryops,* and *Stylogaster.*

The lives of these blind wanderers of the Tropics are very complex and not completely understood. Still, due to detailed studies made by such scientists as T. C. Schneirla and Carl W. Rettenmeyer, we know a great deal about them.

One of the very astonishing things about the army ants, and one that sheds considerable light on their behavior, is the formation of "suicide mills." If a raiding column of army ants should encounter a shower or in some other fashion be separated from the rest, they often begin traveling in a circle. The blind ants, following closely behind each other are unaware that they are not "going somewhere." Around and around the ants go, hour after hour and day after day, until at last

64

most of them die of exhaustion. The survivors from this "suicide mill" eventually wander off, once the chain is broken. They are unthinking, unreasoning little automatons having no ability to break away from instinctive behavior. Once set in motion, the column travels through the jungle hunting game and, under normal conditions, would eventually return to the bivouac site. But if something unusual occurs they are helpless slaves of their instinct to "follow the leader."

The *Ecitons* found here in the United States do not attract the attention of many people. In my many years in the Southeast I have observed their nomadic columns on the move but twice. One such column was seen crossing a little-used drive. The ants continued to move across the concrete in a narrow stream which lasted for several hours. The other case was in my own back yard where I had seated myself one afternoon to enjoy a cup of coffee. While these are the only two instances in which I have actually seen their marching columns, I am sure that they are much more abundant than might be believed. I have often captured large numbers of the winged males and females at insect light traps.

If you were to ask the average person what he considered to be the most vicious creature of Africa, it is probable that he would pick the

Most people do not know that close relatives of the tropical army ants and driver ants occur in the United States. Like their larger and more vicious cousins of the Tropics, these ants (Eciton) *are blind.*

These are the famous driver ants (Dorylus) of Africa, which are closely related to the American army ants. Here we see a marching column of workers protected by large-jawed soldiers along the flanks. These ants live in enormous colonies and will kill and devour any animal unable to escape. They have killed and eaten caged tigers.

lion or, perhaps, the rhinoceros. But he would be ignoring the driver ants *(Dorylus)*, the world's most dangerous animals, even if they are small. These ants are specialists in mass attack and will not hesitate to do battle with any animal, regardless of size. Perhaps we cannot say that these ants are brave, in the sense that a man is brave; they are completely blind and probably do not even know the size of their adversaries. Once, in South Africa, a full-grown leopard confined in a cage was killed by driver ants and its bones picked clean in a single night! They also, sometimes, kill pythons which have recently consumed large meals and become lethargic.

Driver ants have a very disagreeable habit; if a person unknowingly stands in the way of one of their columns, the ants crawl up his legs and then, as if at a given signal, all start biting at the same time.

Like their American relatives, the *Ecitons*, the workers of the

66

African drivers are rather small in size; the smallest workers are hardly over one-eighth inch in length, while the soldiers with their enormous jaws measure almost half an inch. By contrast, the queen is a monster, measuring more than two inches. The winged male looks more like a large hornet than an ant and has eyes, in contrast to the queen who is blind like her workers.

While the raids of the African drivers are, in a way, similar to those of the American army ants, there are some important differences. Apparently, the driver ants have scouts who go out and explore the area, seeking likely places to raid. In this respect, they resemble honeybees which "send" out scouts to locate sources of pollen and nectar. The American army ants do not do this.

Another difference between the American and African warrior ants lies in their way of travel. While the American *Ecitons* move over the surface of the ground, the African *Dorylus* ants may use covered

Note the powerful jaws of this driver ant. Completely blind, it depends on its sensitive antennae to travel and locate game.

earthen runways which they build as they travel along. These underground passages are used mostly during the dry season; with the coming of rains the driver ants move over the surface of the ground.

When ready to go on a raiding safari, the columns move out of the bivouac site, usually about five or six abreast, with the large soldiers stationed along the flanks, their jaws open and ready to defend the hurrying workers. On these raiding expeditions the huge queen does not accompany them, but when the colony is moving to a new location, as they do periodically, the queen is carried or dragged along.

When raiding, the columns hurry along, capturing and devouring anything edible in their path, from a grasshopper to a cow. They invade farms and kill rabbits, poultry, and any other creature that cannot escape their jaws. On the other hand, when these ants invade a native dwelling they flush out and devour all cockroaches, lice, and other pests, leaving the premises completely free of vermin. Seemingly, about the only creatures that successfully escape the jaws of these ants are spiders which suspend themselves from silken threads and in this way outwit their pursuers.

Even though they are blind, the ants shun the direct rays of the sun and, if traveling in sunny weather, usually take advantage of the shade. Usually they stop their march in a sheltered location before dawn. While these ants, like most kinds, are not adapted to aquatic life, they

Like their American cousins, the army ants, African driver ants carry their larvae with them on their travels.

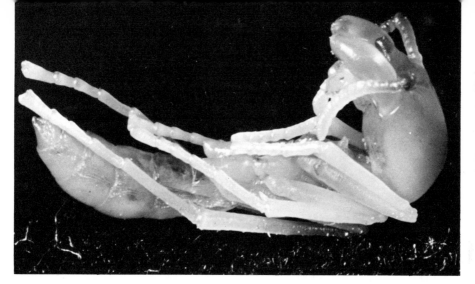

This is a pupal driver ant soldier. When fully developed this pupa will shed its skin and the adult ant will emerge. At first it will be pale in color but will gradually turn black. Such young adults are called callows.

are able to cross small streams. If, in their wanderings, they come to a stream, they pile up in a large mass at the edge. The ants coming up from the rear reinforce those already at the water's edge. Soon the mass of ants becomes so great that it drops onto the water and forms a living rope which extends out across the surface. If the water is not moving rapidly, this chain of ants soon reaches the opposite bank and the march continues. If the stream is moving, the chain is apt to swing about and touch some stick protruding from the opposite bank a little distance downstream. When this occurs, the ants in front grasp this and the column continues on. Not many barriers can stop them, since there are so many of them that sheer numbers usually overcome any obstacle to their progress.

During periods when lowlands are flooded, these ants form themselves into large balls, with their queen and larvae at the center, and float on the surface of the water. Eventually, of course, this ant ball drifts to dry land and the ants resume their normal wanderings. Here in the United States, I have seen both leaf-cutting ants and fire ants do the same thing during floods.

Such are the vicious warrior ants of Africa and tropical America whose armies stream through the jungles devouring any living creature in their paths. They are called driver and army ants with good reason. The driver ants drive all living things before them, and both kinds travel like human armies.

Chapter 5

The Seed Gatherers

We find many parallels between human and ant societies. As hunters, our remote ancestors lived upon the flesh of wild beasts; later, they settled in villages and gathered plants, roots, and seeds. Many human civilizations have grown up and flourished on economies based on rice, wheat, and corn. The seeds of these plants, and others, are highly nutritious and still furnish a large part of our total food supply. Thus, it is not at all surprising to find that several kinds of ants, long ago, began harvesting and storing plant seeds. Such ants occur in many parts of the world, especially the more arid regions. If we attempt to find out why these ants have taken up diets of seeds, it at once becomes obvious that, in addition to being highly nutritious, seeds are available almost everywhere. Large colonies of hunting ants would soon run out of "game," whereas seed-eating ants almost always have abundant supplies of food. On the other hand, seeds are most plentiful in late summer and autumn, so some means of storage becomes a necessity. As we shall see, some ants have solved this problem rather well.

While there are a number of seed-gathering ants, they all belong to one subfamily, the Myrmicinae. Not all these ants feed upon seeds, but the habit occurs in several kinds, including the fire ants (*Solenopsis*), the little harvesters (*Pheidole*), Solomon's ants (*Messor*), the American harvester ants (*Pogonomyrmex*), and others.

The first of all ant studies or observations was made of the seed-gathering ants (*Messor*) of the Mediterranean region. These ants range through Africa southward to the Cape of Good Hope and across southern Asia. Their habits of gathering and storing seeds against times of need were mentioned by many ancient writers, including Aesop, Horace, and Pliny. These are the ants to which King Solomon

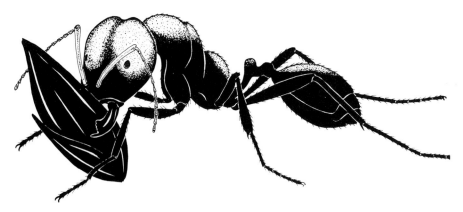

This is the ant which King Solomon and other ancient writers observed in the Holy Land and considered to be an example of industry. It belongs to the genus Messor and is closely related to the seed-harvesting ants (Pogonomyrmex) of our Great Plains.

Here a harvester ant carries a seed into the entrance to its nest. These stores of seeds are often plundered by ground squirrels and other prairie rodents.

referred and which I have called Solomon's ants for convenience. The Latin name *Messor* means "a reaper" and, under feudal law, this was an officer in charge of the harvest. Certainly, this is an appropriate name for these ants which live by harvesting grain.

It is a strange fact that the first modern entomologists doubted the existence of grain-harvesting ants in the Mediterranean area as described by the ancient writers. They considered such ants to be imaginary. It was not until the latter part of the 1880's that the habits of the harvesting ants were studied in detail by such students of ants as J. T. Moggridge of Europe and Henry C. McCook of the United States. It was such people as these who definitely proved that the ancient writers had been correct in their observations. We may perhaps pause to wonder why it was that the ancient observers knew so much about ants. But since they lived close to nature they were probably more conscious of the natural world about them.

In June, 1829, Lieutenant-Colonel W. H. Sykes, then serving in India, became interested in seed-storing ants he saw on the parade ground at Poona. He noticed that these ants, after rains, carried out their stores of seeds to dry in the sun. Later, he saw the ants carrying the seeds back into the nests. Sykes was probably the first modern observer to become convinced that ants do harvest and store plant seeds. While the ants he saw at Poona were *Pheidole providens* and not the *Messor* ants of King Solomon's time, Lieutenant-Colonel Sykes definitely proved that ants do gather and store seeds. If any doubt remained it was removed by Moggridge who studied, in detail, the habits of *Messor* ants in southern France in 1871 and 1872. Here he watched the busy ants collecting seeds and carrying them into their nests. He also excavated the nests and saw the filled grain bins. In addition, he identified the seeds and determined that they came from plants of eighteen different families growing in the vicinity. One other interesting observation he made: he saw that the ants bit off the germ ends of the seeds which would prevent their germination in the damp underground bins. This was something that such ancient writers as Pliny had stated. However, it seems to be a point that is as yet unsettled. Certainly, the American harvesters do not take this precaution, as I have proved to my own satisfaction by removing seeds from the bins and growing them in pots. Still, it is possible, or even probable, that some of the Old World harvesters do cut out the germ ends of the seeds.

If you have ever traveled across the Great Plains of the United States you have no doubt seen the nests of the American harvesters (*Pogonomyrmex*). They are quite conspicuous features of the plains, each nest cone surrounded by a circular space which is completely bare of vegetation. The nests are very uniform in shape; each one is a neat, sandy cone often more than two feet high. This realm of the harvester ants is level or rolling plain covered by low shrubs and sparce grasses. In spring, the blooms of prairie flowers nestle close to the ground, brought into being by rains which sweep across the landscape. In late summer, the prairies become dry, parched by the sun and the hot winds. These heated winds create spinning "dust devils" which dance over the prairie like twisting columns of smoke carrying dust high in the sky. By then the prairie plants have shed their seeds and their dry leaves rattle in the breezes. On the prairie these two seasons,

Western harvester ants build large conical mounds of sand and gravel on the prairies, with the entrance to the underground chambers on one side. These mounds are surrounded by large, bare areas fringed with various plants growing from seeds accidentally dropped by the ants or from sprouting seeds which have been discarded.

spring and autumn, are the times when wild creatures as well as plants are most active. The same conditions affect the ants that dwell there. In summer, no small creature could long survive the mid-day heat of the hot sand, so most of them seek shelter beneath the surface where it is cool and damp.

There are several different kinds of harvester ants. The most widely distributed one is *Pogonomyrmex occidentalis* which ranges from Canada southward to Arizona. This is the ant which Dr. McCook called the occidental or "western" ant, and it is its nests which are so conspicuous on the high plains. The second most abundant western harvester is *Pogonomyrmex barbatus* which Dr. McCook called the "agricultural" ant. Why he called it this we shall see later. This ant ranges from Colorado southward into Texas and Mexico. While most of the harvester ants dwell in arid or semiarid regions, there is one kind which ranges down through southeastern United States where the climate is humid. This latter kind is *Pogonomyrmex badius* and is the only harvester ant found east of the Mississippi River. Other, closely related harvester ants are found in California. The habits of all these ants are quite similar, although there are some differences in their nests and in their manner of harvesting seeds.

My own experience with *Pogomonyrmex* ants was gained by several trips across Colorado and Wyoming where I excavated their nests and studied their habits. I have also studied the habits of the eastern harvesters in Florida and other southeastern locations. On the High Plains, the nests of the harvesters are not at all difficult to find; one can easily spot them from the highways where they appear as large, bare patches in the prairie vegetation. Usually these bare patches or ant "courtyards" are about ten feet in diameter, but those of the agricultural harvester may extend to thirty-five feet. On approaching one of these colonies, the observer is at once impressed by its extreme neatness. At the center is the perfectly formed cone of sand or fine gravel. Surrounding this is a circular space completely bare of all vegetation. Apparently, the industrious ants cut down any plant that takes root there. At the outer edge of this "courtyard" there is usually a fringing zone of grasses and weeds which, it might appear, had been planted by the ants. Indeed, one early observer, Gideon Lincecum, was led to believe that the ants

74

These are seeds from the grain bin in a harvester ant nest. Most of the seeds are those of paspalum *grass which was abundant in the vicinity of the nest.*

had actually planted seeds around the nests so they would have nearby sources of grain. Mr. Lincecum, as well as some other early students of ants, believed that they planted seeds of *Aristida* grass around their nests and thus they called this grass "ant rice." While this makes an interesting little story, we now know that it is not true. It is a fact, however, that harvester ants may accidentally drop seeds near their nests and these often grow into plants, but most of the plants that grow around ant courtyards have another origin. Harvester ants gather seeds from nearly all the plants growing in the vicinity and these are carried into the nest and stored in underground chambers or "bins." It is but natural that, under the moist conditions which often prevail in the nests, the seeds may sprout. At least, this is what occurs in American harvester ant nests. Sprouting seeds are of no use to the ants so they are carried out of the nest and discarded around the outer edge of the courtyard. If weather conditions are favorable, these sprouting seeds take root and grow, but it was not the ants' "intention" to actually plant them; it was done by accident.

If we closely examine several of these ant nests, we find that they follow a basic "plan." The conical mound, as we have seen, is placed at the exact center of the courtyard with the gate or entrance in one side of the cone near the bottom, usually on the southern or eastern side. Peering into this entrance, it can be seen that the passage leads downward at a steep angle. The cleared, circular courtyard surrounding the cone is of hard-packed earth and around the edges of this bare disc is a rather dense growth of plants. Now, if one looks closely, it will be noticed that the ground among these fringing plants is strewn with seed husks or chaff. Many of the seeds carried into the nest are still enclosed in their husks. Within the nest, these are removed and carried out and discarded, which accounts for the accumulation of husks at the edge of the courtyard. Also discarded in these trash dumps are sprouting and damaged seeds, as well as insect remains such as beetle wing-covers. The truth is that, while harvester ants feed mostly upon seeds, they also capture and devour many insects. Probably this is a carry-over from the carnivorous habits of their ancestors.

The interior architecture of a prairie harvester "city" is most interesting and its size is a tribute to the industrious insects that created it. The excavation of such a nest is very laborious and not without its hazards, since these ants sting severely. Anyone who has done such excavation work can sympathize with the victims of the ancient Mexican Indians who, it is said, sometimes tortured enemies by binding their hands and feet and placing them near harvester ant nests!

In eastern Colorado I excavated a large harvester ant nest in order to study its inhabitants. With a spade I first cut away one side of the nest cone to reveal the chambers and passages which penetrated all parts. The chambers, arranged one above the other, were from three to six inches wide and up to an inch from floor to ceiling. The floors were of hard-packed earth, as a result of the hurrying feet of the ants going to and fro on their errands. The chambers near the top of the cone were filled with white larval and pupal ants, and when the nest was opened the workers swarmed out and carried these young into the deeper passages where they were lost to view. Ants by the hundreds also swarmed out across the bare courtyard and I could only avoid being stung by continually stamping my boots to dislodge the ants.

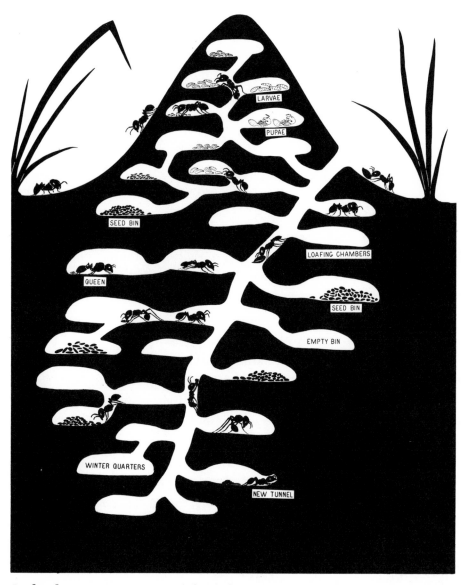

In this drawing we see most of the daily activities that go on in a harvester ant nest. In the chambers above ground are larvae and pupae. Farther down are chambers filled with stored seeds. At the left is the royal chamber where the queen is laying eggs. The cold months of winter are spent in hibernation in the deepest chambers.

Continuing my excavation downward beneath the nest cone, I found more chambers, all connected by passages or tunnels. Some of these chambers contained stores of seeds, while others contained young ants.

This close-up of a harvester nest chamber shows an adult ant with several pupae and larvae.

Many chambers were empty or, apparently, served as resting places for the inhabitants. My spade exposed tier after tier of chambers as I dug deeper, and now and then I came to filled seed-storage bins. Contained in these bins were seeds of great variety; it is probable that seeds of almost all the local plants were represented. In a few bins I noticed sprouting seeds. How far down into the ground the chambers and tunnels extended I do not know because I did not reach the "basement" of this ant city. Dr. McCook, who completely excavated such an ant nest, found that it extended more than eight feet below the surface and that seeds were stored in even the deepest chambers. In these lowest chambers he also found many callow ants, or pale adults, which had only recently changed into the mature stage.

In winter, the ants retire to the deepest chambers for hibernation. Here, far below the frost line, they are safe from winter's cold. The depth to which harvester ants excavate their passages varies with the kind of ant. A nest of the agricultural harvester (*P. barbatus*) which was excavated in Arizona contained 436 chambers, some as deep as fifteen feet! The underground nest area was seven feet in diameter and was inhabited by a total of 12,358 ants. (Just how Mr. E. G. Davis, the investigator, was able to make such an exact count is difficult to understand. When a nest is opened the ants swarm out and rapidly crawl everywhere, including over the person of the investigator. Certainly, Mr. Davis must have been very busy!)

Such is the inner structure, or plan, of these amazing ant cities where thousands of inhabitants live and toil in darkness, continually digging new passages, husking seeds and rearing young. In the royal chamber, hidden deep within the nest, the queen lays eggs. A harvester ant colony is forever growing. As workers die or are captured by enemies they must be replaced and it is the queen's duty to supply the eggs for the production of this labor force.

A harvester ant colony is a well-regulated society where there is a division of various duties among the inhabitants. Some ants toil in the dark underground chambers, husking seeds and carrying out the chaff; others dig new tunnels and chambers. How they "decide" where to dig we do not know. In an artificial nest between panes of glass, these ants are forever digging. When they run out of space to dig new chambers they fill in old ones and dig again. It seems as if some instinct

In the royal chamber we see the queen (left) and a worker. Notice the queen's large thorax or mid-section which once had wings attached. After mating she broke off her wings since they were of no further use to her in the underground nest which she founded.

drives them to dig, regardless of the need for more space. They are industrious little workers. Like tiny dogs, they use their front feet to loosen the grains of sand which are then brushed back out of the way. Sometimes their jaws are employed as well. They are always in a great hurry, as if the chamber had to be finished within a given time.

Some kinds of harvester ants, in addition to the usual workers, have a big-headed soldier caste. This is true of the southeastern harvester (*P. badius*). Just what the duties of these individuals are is not known for sure; perhaps they have no real duties and are really relics of the ancient days when their ancestors lived by the hunt. Certainly, they wander about the vicinity of the nest as if looking for something useful to do, but uncertain as to just what. It is believed, however, by most authorities that these soldier ants use their large jaws to husk seeds and perhaps to cut up hard seeds. For this reason they are sometimes called "millers."

In feeding on seeds, the ants rasp away the starchy material with their filelike tongues and this is eaten or fed to the young or to the queen. When feeding, the ants often "sit down," so to speak, with their abdomens bent forward beneath their bodies and their four hind legs resting on the ground. The front legs are used to help hold the seed as it is fed upon. If one has the patience, it is not difficult to observe these ants in the act of eating in an artificial nest of the "ant farm" type. Under natural conditions this takes place only in the underground chambers and is never seen by human eyes.

All ants have definite food preferences and this is certainly true of the harvesters. I once poured a spoonful of honey on the ground near a harvester colony to see if they would eat it. At first they gathered around and seemed to be tasting it, but I soon found that they were carrying sand and covering it up. They scraped together grains of sand with their front legs and jaws and then, using their abdomens to help hold it, carried the sand and dumped it on the honey. Apparently, the

This excavated harvester ant nest shows how the underground chambers are arranged one above the other. In the upper chambers are large-headed "miller" ants and workers in the seed bins. Chambers at the bottom contain white larval and pupal ants. Tunnels lead from one chamber to another.

Harvester ants often assume this strange pose while sunning themselves outside their nests.

Here a harvester ant drags a large stone. These ants can easily lift objects fifty times their own weight.

ants realized that the sticky honey constituted a danger, so they took steps to cover it up. Later, I was interested to read that Moggridge, nearly a hundred years previously, had seen European harvesters (*Messor* ants) doing the same thing.

While we can never see into the dark passages and chambers of the underground ant city without disturbing the normal routine of the ants, we can easily observe most of their daily activities above ground. We can see them carrying sand and stones out of the nest and placing them upon the cone. In this way, gravel and sand from considerable depths are brought to the surface. It is said that prospectors for precious stones and minerals sometimes examine these ant mounds for evidence of underground deposits. Particles of fine gold have been seen among the gravel on harvester cones, and I have sometimes seen small garnets. For such work as carrying stones, the ants use their jaws and they can carry quite heavy loads. I once weighed a harvester ant and found that the stone it had carried out of its nest weighed more than fifty times its own weight!

In watching these busy ants at work there seems to be much confusion and aimless running about. One wonders how they ever accomplish anything. If we follow an ant as it walks about the courtyard, it usually seems to be undecided as to where to go. It may pick up a pebble and carry it for a foot or so and then drop it. I have seen an ant carry a stone into the nest while others were busily carrying stones out of the nest. Still, in spite of all this disorder, life goes on and the nest is built and provisioned with seeds. Actually, these ants have rather definite daily routines. About dusk each evening the outside entrance to the nest is closed or barricaded with pebbles, just as we close and lock our doors each night. Any ants still out foraging in the surrounding area are locked out. In closing the entrance, the ants push sand and pebbles into the opening from the inside, while one or two ants remain outside to complete the job by piling sand into the depression. Dr. McCook, who observed this process in detail, failed to determine what happened to the ants who locked themselves outside. Perhaps they were forced to spend the night in the open. The nests are also closed before rain storms and during winter.

Prairie harvesters are late sleepers; they do not begin opening their

In this view a harvester ant's "beard" can be seen. (Its scientific name, Pogonomyrmex, *means "bearded ant.") These hairs, called* ammochaets, *are found
on the "chins" of many desert ants and are believed by some authorities to serve
as brushes to clean dust and sand from the combs on their forelegs. These
combs, one of which is seen on the foreleg of this ant, are used to clean the
sensitive antennae. Other authorities believe these hairs protect the ants' delicate mouth parts from blowing sand.*

nests until about 9:00 A.M. The pebbles blocking the gate are removed
from the inside and the first ant looks cautiously out upon the new day.
If all looks serene, she emerges and carries the removed stones an inch
or so away and drops them. After a few minutes, more ants emerge
and soon large numbers are hurrying across the courtyard and into
the surrounding vegetation. Here they follow well-beaten trails leading
away from the nest. These trails are foraging paths and it is over these
that harvested seeds and other foods are carried home. While the
prairie harvesters use trails, these paths are not nearly as well defined
as are those of the agricultural harvesters found farther south. Unlike
ants of most other kinds, harvester ants lay no scent trails. If a worker
finds a good source of food, such as a plant with many seeds, she picks
up a seed or cuts it from the plant and carries it home, but she does not

leave scent patches upon the ground for other ants to follow. Probably this instinct has never been developed in these ants who dwell in sandy areas where blowing sand would soon obliterate such trails. Apparently, harvester ants learn to recognize conspicuous landmarks in the vicinities of their nests and can find their way home when picked up and moved a short distance away.

In gathering seeds, there are some differences in habits among the various kinds of ants. The prairie harvesters actually climb up on plants and cut off the seeds, while the southeastern harvesters seem satisfied to pick them up from the ground where they have fallen.

Just how far these industrious ants travel away from their nests to gather food is unknown, but it is probable that they range as far as fifty or more feet, which is a considerable distance when the size of the ants is considered. Dr. McCook observed a worker that had picked up a seed thirty feet from its nest and found that it arrived back at the nest within two minutes. He estimated that, by comparison with a man, the ant was traveling at about twenty-one miles an hour!

As to the quantity of grain stored by a large harvester colony, it seems possible that the amount may reach at least a quart or so. In visiting many prairie harvester colonies I was rather amazed at the number which had been plundered of their stores by kangaroo rats and other prairie rodents. To such seed-eating animals, the ant grain bins are an irresistible temptation.

Probably the most spectacular event in the otherwise routine life of a harvester colony is the swarming of newly emerged queens and males. These winged individuals are produced in summer and, when the time is right, they swarm out of the nest in great numbers. They crawl up on weeds and grasses and eventually fly off. Mating apparently occurs in flight, after which the males die. The mated queens remove their wings by pulling them off with their jaws or by rubbing them against rocks or sticks. Each queen then excavates a hole in the earth about ten inches deep, at the bottom of which she digs several small chambers. She now plugs up the entrance hole and lays a cluster of about fifty eggs. When these hatch into larvae they are fed on secretions from her own body. In time, these larvae change into adult workers, but they are smaller in size than those that will be produced later

Harvester ants gather seeds from the surrounding area and carry them into the underground chambers where they are stored in bins. This one carries a dandelion seed with its attached parachute.

due to the small amount of food the queen is able to give them. If all goes well, the new queendom prospers and gradually the colony increases in size. It is a sad fact, however, that only a very few queens are successful in starting new colonies. In the case of the agricultural harvester, it was found that about a thousand new colonies were started per acre of land, but a later examination showed that not a single one had survived the summer! This small percentage of nest establishment no doubt accounts for the enormous number of queens that are produced.

The vast plains where the harvesters dwell constitute a harsh environment where only the strongest and best adapted can survive. This was once the home of the buffalo and wandering Indian tribes, but they are gone. It is now populated by jackrabbits that emerge from their hiding places at dusk to feed, and by range cattle that graze quietly on the prairie grasses. Many of the native prairie inhabitants have disappeared, but the harvester ants still live as they have lived for a million years or more; their ways of life have not changed.

Chapter 6

The Mushroom Growers

THE STUDY OF PLANTS and animals has led me into many strange situations and places, but the one that I recall most vividly was the night I sat beside a column of leaf-cutting ants deep in a Louisiana forest. Earlier in the evening I had encountered a black wolf, but when I at last located the column of ants I had come to study, the wolf was quickly forgotten. The ants were following a narrow trail across the forest floor beneath tall, long-leaf pines and I set up my camera and electronic lights to photograph them. The path followed by the ants was well marked and had been cleared of pine needles. It was about two inches wide.

In the beam of my flashlight I watched the ants as they came into view out of the darkness and disappeared twenty feet away behind the trunk of a large pine. I could see that almost every ant carried a leaf fragment over its head. These fragments, or sections, which had been cut out of leaves, were carried vertically in the ants' jaws and as the column of leaf-carrying ants streamed along they reminded me of a long, green snake crawling over the ground. Not every ant carried a load; some walked along empty-handed, as if they had merely come along for the trip. However, they all hurried down the path as if on important business that could not wait. When I turned my light onto the advancing ants each one seemed to have a headlight. Soon, however, this minor mystery was solved. The light was being reflected from the polished front edges of their sharp jaws.

These amazing ants were leaf-cutting ants *(Atta texana)* which range up out of Mexico, across Texas, and into Louisiana. It was in the lush, semitropical forests of southern Louisiana that I had chosen to study them. These ants are close relatives of the famous leaf-cutting, or para-

For compost upon which to grow their special fungus, the Atta ants collect pieces of leaves which they carry into their nests.

The Attas carry their leaves over well-established ant paths through the forest. These ant highways are usually quite distinct and can be followed long distances.

sol, ants of Central and South America which often defoliate trees and damage gardens. In South America they are known as *saubas*. People are often surprised to learn that true leaf-cutting ants are found here in our own country.

The day after my nocturnal observations I returned to the scene and found the ant trail deserted. While these ants usually work at night, they sometimes forage for leaves during daylight hours, especially during cloudy weather. I traced the narrow ant path away through the forest and found that the ants had been cutting leaves from a chinquapin tree. Almost every leaf had small sections neatly cut out. When I followed the trail in the other direction I found that, about a hundred feet away, it disappeared into a tunnel almost an inch in diameter. A short distance farther, near the edge of the forest, I discovered the

The entrance to the Attas' *underground ant "city" is about an inch in diameter. Note the freshly excavated pellets of damp sand.*

Leaf-cutting ants (Atta) live deep in the ground where they excavate large chambers in which they grow fungus gardens. Sometimes these underground "mushroom cellars" are as deep as twenty feet.

surface mounds of sand which marked the location of the underground nest cavities.

There were dozens of these mounds, each of which was about a foot in diameter and about six inches high. They were shaped somewhat like miniature volcanic craters with their inner walls sloping downward to the entrances which led to the underground chambers. These mounds covered an area nearly fifty feet in diameter and, from the tremendous amount of sand which had been brought to the surface, it was evident that there must be large underground cavities or "ant caves" beneath my feet. I found no surface ant trails leading away from the area, but I had not expected to find any since these crafty ants usually build underground "feeder" tunnels which extend away, just beneath the surface, for nearly a hundred feet before emerging. It is through these tunnels that the ants pass on their way to and from leaf-harvesting sites.

I had recruited some men with shovels and they set to work digging downward through the sandy soil. The digging was easy and within a few minutes the workmen had reached a point about five feet below the surface. I had them cut away a vertical wall and then begin removing soil a little at a time as we approached the point where I believed the underground chambers to be located.

At last, one of the shovels broke into one of the cavities and when I carefully dug away the earth with a trowel, a large, oval cavity about ten inches high and nearly two feet long was exposed. Out of this cavity the angry ants swarmed by the hundreds but, fortunately for us, they had no stings. Even so, their sharp jaws can draw blood. The cavity which was exposed by our labors was well worth the effort. Its entire lower portion was filled with a gray, spongy material which, in a general way, resembled a honeycomb. This was one of the fungus gardens of the *Atta* colony. Peering closely at this mass I could see that, in addition to the normal-sized ants I had seen the night before, there were hundreds of very tiny ants busily at work in the fungal mass. These were the gardeners and weeders whose duty is caring for the growing fungus or mushroom garden. The field ants make daily (or nightly) forays out into the surrounding forest to gather leaf sections

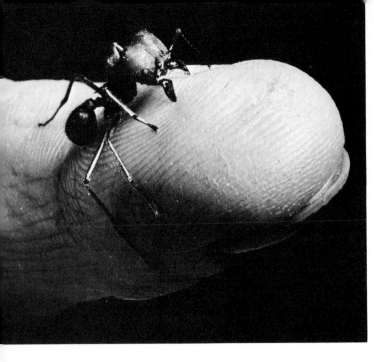

Atta *workers have no stings, but they can draw blood with their sharp jaws.*

This is the honeycombed mass of fungus from an Atta *chamber. The shovel on which it rests gives an idea of its size.*

which are brought into the subterranean cavities and used as a medium upon which fungus is grown for food.

In their leaf-harvesting operations, the ants climb the trees and either cut sections out of the leaves with their sharp jaws or clip the leaves off and allow them to fall to the ground. Here, other ants cut out sections and carry them off. These leaf fragments are quite heavy when we consider the size of the ants that carry them. Dr. Frank E. Lutz found that the leaves carried by the Panama leaf-cutters (*Atta cephalotes*) weighed eight times as much as the ants themselves. This might be compared to a man carrying 1,000 pounds!

In his book on jungle adventure, *Living Treasure*, Ivan T. Sanderson makes some interesting comparisons of leaf-cutting ants and men. In British Honduras, Mr. Sanderson estimated that the leaves carried by the ants weighed only *twice* as much as the ants. This, however, is still quite a heavy load. He found that the ants were cutting leaves from the top of a tree a hundred feet tall and carrying them back to their nest located 300 feet away. By comparing the stride of the ants to that of man, he estimated that they traveled a total distance of twenty-one and a half miles. Remember too that, on the return journey, each ant carried twice its own weight. In addition to this, the ants had to climb a 100-foot tree, which is comparable to a man climbing Mount Everest. They then carried their heavy loads down "Mount Everest" and on to their nest. Mr. Sanderson marked some of these toiling ants and found that some individuals made the round trip *twice* during one night!

In the nest, the bits of leaves are cut up into small pieces and placed about in the mass. Upon each piece, a "start" of fungus is planted. In addition to cultivating this fungus growth, these tiny workers or *minims* must be continually "weeding" out foreign fungi. It is only natural that the "field hands" should accidentally bring in large numbers of fungus spores along with leaf bits. If not carefully removed from the pure culture of ant fungus, these foreign fungus "weeds" would contaminate it. The ants do not feed upon any fungus except their own special kind and this ant fungus grows nowhere except in their underground cavities.

Since most ants have no "voices," I was rather amazed when I picked up one of the large workers between my fingers and heard a rather loud

Like all ants, the Attas can carry heavy loads. This Atta ant transports a large section which it cut from a leaf with its scissor-like jaws.

Leaf-cutting ants often cut sections from leaves a considerable distance from their nests. Shown here are the large leaf-cutters of Brazil (Atta laevigata).

In this close-up we see Atta *ants toiling in their fungus garden. The gray fungus mycelia grows upon bits of leaves carried in by foraging ants. Note that there are ants of various sizes. The smallest workers are "weeders" who must continually remove foreign fungi to keep the culture pure.*

squeeking sound. These ants have well-developed sound-making or *stridulating* organs located at the base of the abdomen and consisting of a file and a scraper. How these organs serve the ants is unknown; perhaps they are alarm signals used by the ants in the dark subterranean passages where they make their homes.

The relationships between fungus-growing ants and their fungi have puzzled biologists for a long while. As long as the ants are in control of the fungus it does not produce fruiting bodies and spores. The ants propogate it vegetatively, just as we often grow flowering plants from "slips" or cuttings. As we shall see later, there are a number of kinds of fungus-growing ants, but all the fungi grown by them are apparently "mushrooms." In other words, all these fungi would, if left to themselves, mature and eventually form typical mushrooms. Actually, this sometimes occurs when an *Atta* colony dies or moves away. In a few such cases, large mushrooms have appeared, having developed from abandoned ant fungus gardens. Thus, it is known that all the fungi cultivated by ants belong to the *Agaricaceae*, which includes the mushrooms, toadstools, and puffballs. So we can truthfully say that these ants are "mushroom growers."

Now, in order to properly classify or identify a fungus, a botanist must see its fruiting stage. Since these ant fungi do not normally mature to this stage, most of them have remained unclassified until recently. Dr. Neal A. Weber of Swarthmore College has been successful in cultivating the fungi from various fungus-growing ants on artificial media in his laboratory. These fungi have, in some cases, produced the typical mushroom stages in Dr. Weber's laboratory and enabled him to classify them. The artificial media used by Dr. Weber for growing ant fungus was similar to those used for bacterial cultures. They consisted of potato-dextrose, malt extract-peptone-dextrose, and other media.

In his experiments, Dr. Weber placed small bits of foreign fungus in the garden of a fungus-growing ant and then observed the results. Within a few minutes the ants discovered the foreign fungus and, after tasting it, carried it away and discarded it. Here we have proof that foreign fungi are carefully weeded out of fungus gardens to assure that they remain pure.

Within about forty hours after the bits of leaves are planted with fungus they become covered with a whitish growth of *mycelium,* or fungus threads. This fungus requires very special conditions of moisture and temperature, and these are carefully controlled by the ants. The marvelous thing is that the ants are able to maintain these exacting conditions without the aid of such instruments as thermostats and hygrostats which we would use. They do this in a number of ways. For example, leaves are harvested only at night, or on cloudy days during hot, dry weather. Wet leaves are never carried into the fungus cellars. During periods of unusually dry weather, the outside entrances are closed to conserve moisture. When the fungus gardens become too damp, ventilating tunnels are opened. I once attempted to maintain an *Atta* fungus garden in a glass container, but I could never regulate the temperature and humidity so as to keep it flourishing in the way it did in the ants' underground chambers.

It may seem strange that certain ants have taken up the culture of fungi, while no ant has ever actually developed the habit of growing

Here is the winged queen of Atta laevigata *of Brazil, the world's largest leafcutters. This queen is more than an inch long.*

seed-bearing plants. If we give the matter some thought, however, we soon realize how the habit probably began. It seems likely that these ants originally lived in underground nests just as they do now. Beneath the surface of the earth is the normal location for the growth of the fungal strands, or *mycelia,* of mushrooms. No doubt this fungus growth often invaded the ants' nest areas and tunnels, so it required only a short step for them to begin feeding upon it and, eventually, to cultivate it. As a result, these ants began the cultivation of their fungus "gardens" many millions of years before man took up the growing of any food crop.

If the ant fungus garden is closely examined under a hand lens, it can be seen that it consists of minute, threadlike strands of the fungus mycelia with, here and there, small whitish clumps. These clumps are called *bromatia,* or kohlrabi heads, and it is upon these that the ants feed. Strangely, the fungus produces these *bromatia* only when under cultivation by the ants. Evidently the ants do something to the growing fungus which causes it to produce these special "fruiting" bodies which constitute their food.

After opening the first chamber in the *Atta* colony in Louisiana, we continued our excavation and located about a dozen others which varied in size from six inches to more than a foot in diameter. All were shaped more or less like watermelons and were interconnected by passages. Here and there, tunnels extended upward to the surface. The deepest chamber was about six feet below the surface, but other investigators have found them as deep as twenty feet! Each cavity was filled with fungus within which were numerous white larval and pupal ants. Adult ants were present in enormous numbers in all the chambers. How many ants are there in such a colony? No one, as far as I know, has ever made a count, but I am sure that a large colony may contain several million individuals.

In southern Louisiana, the large colonies with their numerous surface craters are called "ant towns," and the ants themselves are known locally as "town ants." In Texas they are called "cut ants," probably because of their leaf-cutting habits. In areas where they are abundant they are serious pests, since they may defoliate a tree or ruin a garden in one night. Also, they often carry off other things besides leaves to be

98

A Trachymyrmex *worker in its fungus garden. Notice the white cottony fungus. The ants feed upon special "fruiting" bodies, called* bromatia, *which grow on the fungus.*

This is all that remains of tree leaves after the leaf-cutting ants have cut sections from them.

used as compost for mushroom gardens. One Louisiana farmer told me that a busy column of these ants once emptied an entire sack of chicken feed in one night!

The founding of an *Atta* colony follows, in general, that of most other earth-inhabiting ants. At certain seasons, usually from April to July, the winged males and queens swarm out of the colonies. Usually this occurs at night, especially after heavy rains have fallen. They are often attracted to bright lights in large numbers; at a service station located a short distance from a large ant colony, piles of dead males and queens often accumulate. The actual flights usually begin at almost exactly 3:40 A.M. and continue until 4:10 which is about daybreak.

An Atta *queen (left) is very large in comparison to her workers. Notice her large thorax which once had wings attached. After mating, she severed her wings and settled down to an underground existence where her sole duty is the laying of eggs.*

Trachymyrmex *queens lay their eggs in the fungus garden where their larvae are also kept.*

While most of the queens that leave the nests on nuptial flights come to sad ends, a very few live to mate and establish colonies. Previous to leaving the parent nest, each queen fills her mouth with fungus from the fungus garden. This is the dowery she takes out into the world with her to found her queendom. After mating, she selects a spot on the ground, cuts off her wings, and begins digging a hole a few inches deep. A small cavity is excavated at the lower end of the shaft and the entrance is then sealed, after which she retires to the underground chamber. First, she spits out the start of fungus she had the foresight to bring with her and then fertilizes it with material from her own body. The tiny bit of fungus begins to grow and she carefully tends it. Soon she lays a few eggs and, later, places some of them within the mass of growing fungus. (A few of the eggs she eats!) In time, the remaining eggs hatch into larval ants which are fed on the fungus. Eventually, these larvae transform into pupae and then into adults. The outside entrance is now opened and bits of leaves carried in to nourish the fungus garden. From then on, if all goes well, the colony will grow as more and more workers are produced and more, and larger, chambers are excavated and additional fungus gardens started. It is not known how long a queen lives, but it is certain that the colony exists far beyond the life of the original queen. This is possible be-

Here a Trachymyrmex *nest has been excavated in order to photograph the fungus cavity seen at the right. The outside entrance to the nest was almost directly above the fungus cavity, which was about eight inches below the surface of the ground.*

OPPOSITE: *A close-up of the fungus cavity. Note how the masses of gray fungus are suspended from small roots which penetrate the cavity.*

cause newly mated queens are adopted into the colony as time goes on.

When an *Atta* nest is opened and we see the masses of gray fungus with, here and there, bits of leaves planted in it, it seems obvious that the ants are cultivating fungus for food. But perhaps this is because we already know about their habits. The first naturalists to see these remarkable ants and to observe their leaf-collecting habits were completely at a loss to explain what use they made of the leaves. The first person to study the Texas leaf-cutters *(Atta texana)* was Professor S. B. Buckley who recorded his observations in the Proceedings of the Academy of Natural Sciences of Philadelphia in 1860. Like other early naturalists, he failed to realize what use the ants made of the leaves. It was believed that they were carried into the *Atta* nests and used to line the chambers. One writer stated that the leaves were used to thatch the nest domes, thereby protecting the young ants from deluging rains. In other words, the leaves were used as a sort of wallpaper! It remained for Thomas Belt, who conducted many investigations of the tropical plants and animals of Central America, to discover the truth about these ants. His observations were recorded in his book, *The Naturalist in Nicaragua* (1874). Mr. Belt, too, was at first mystified as to use of the leaves, but when he excavated a colony and found the masses of fungus, it gradually dawned on him that the ants were

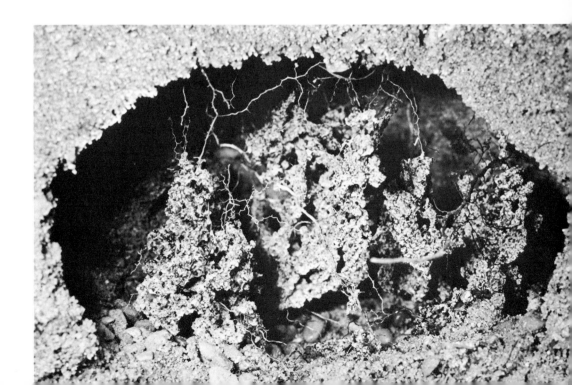

Close-up of hanging fungus masses in a Trachymyrmex *nest. Note fragments of leaves at bottom which have been carried in by the ants.*

using the leaves as a sort of compost upon which to grow fungus. He reported, "Some naturalists have supposed that they used them [the leaves] directly as food; others, that they roof their underground nests with them. I believe the real use they make of them is as a manure, on which grows a minute species of fungus, on which they feed—that they are, in reality, mushroom growers and eaters." Later naturalists doubted the truth of Mr. Belt's statements, since it seemed too incredible to believe that the ants actually cultivated mushrooms in their underground cellars. Now, of course, we know that Belt was correct with respect to the *Atta* ants, and that other ants, too, keep fungus gardens.

So far we have been talking about the large leaf-cutting ants *(Atta)* which occur in Central and South America and northward into Texas and Louisiana. You may be surprised to learn that fungus-growing ants of other kinds are found in many other parts of the United States, and that some of them range all the way to Canada. While the habits of these ants are not as spectacular as those of the large leaf-cutters, they are true fungus-growers and many of their habits are just as interesting.

104

Probably the most common of these little fungus-growers are those having the long scientific name of *Trachymyrmex septentrionalis* and which range over most of the eastern United States. Related kinds are found in the Southwest. Some kinds of these miniature fungus-growers cut leaves, like their larger relatives the *Atta* ants, but most of them collect caterpillar droppings, fallen flower petals, and other vegetable materials. I have also seen them carrying fallen huckleberry blooms into their nests. My own experience with these little ants has been gained by studying them in a sandy area along the Luxapililla River in the Southeast over a period of many years. They are timid little creatures that never make the slightest effort to defend themselves. In fact, when disturbed, they "play possum." Little more than an eighth of an inch long, their bodies are covered with tiny spines and, since their bodies are not shiny, they are rather difficult to see as they walk slowly along in the grass or carry sand out of their tiny nests. The only surface indication of one of these nests is a small streak of sand which has been carried out of the tunnel and discarded. Usually the entrance to the

Another worker tending its fungus garden. Notice that the ant's body is covered with warts and spines. These ants are less than one-eighth inch long and move slowly.

underground nest is located several inches away from the sandpile, so
it is only after some experience that one learns just where to look for it.
When one of the tunnels is located it is not at all difficult to find the
underground chambers where the fungus gardens are located. Usually
it is best to commence digging a few inches away and then to work
gradually toward the spot where it is expected that the chamber is to
be found. Usually, the tunnel goes straight down so the location of the
chamber is not difficult to guess at. As a general rule, the first chamber
will be found about six inches below the surface and will be about the
size of a large orange. Other, similar, chambers may often be encountered below the first one. The fungus garden is blue-gray in color and
usually hangs suspended from small plant roots extending across the
chambers. Like their larger cousins, the leaf-cutters, these ants practice
a type of climate control in their nests, since their fungus gardens are
sensitive to temperature and humidity. There are two seasons when the
entrances to the nests are open and when there is surface activity.
These are spring and autumn; during mid-summer, when hot, dry
weather prevails, the entrances are closed, making the colonies quite
difficult to find.

*Fungus-growing ants of
several kinds are found in
the United States. This
drawing shows a cross-sec-
tion through a* Trachymyrmex *ant nest. The large
cavity, about three inches
in diameter, contains the
growing masses of fungus
suspended from plant roots.
The small enlargement in
the tunnel near the en-
trance was the original cavity excavated by the queen
when she established the
colony.*

Trachymyrmex *worker carrying fragment of an oak leaf down a twig to its nest to be used for growing fungus.*

Since *Trachymyrmex* colonies are never large, only a few ants will be found working in the fungus garden. Seemingly, small, newly formed colonies use only caterpillar droppings and other vegetable debris for fertilizing their mushroom gardens. I have never found these ants actually cutting and carrying leaf fragments into their nests, except in the case of older, well-established colonies. The most interesting case was that of a colony located about two feet from a small oak whose leaves were young and tender. The ants were busy climbing up the stem of the oak and out on its leaves where they were cutting out small pieces with their sharp jaws. Usually these pieces were circular or semicircular in shape and, after being cut out, were carried down the stem. Like the tropical leaf-cutters, they carried the leaf fragments over their heads.

107

In many cases, these little leaf-cutters stood on the portion of the leaf being snipped out, with the result that both ant and leaf fragment tumbled to the ground. Here, the ant scurried about until it had located its bit of leaf. Usually it had some difficulty in getting its heavy load hoisted over its back so that it could be carried back to the nest.

Unlike *Atta* fungus gardens, I have never had any difficulty in keeping one of these *Trachymyrmex* gardens and its inhabitants in a glass container. By supplying the ants with finely chopped-up leaves or rose petals, they kept their garden growing as well as when it was located in the ground. Within this fungus garden, the queen laid eggs which developed into larval ants. One such colony remained healthy in my studio for many months.

While the fungus-growing ants discussed above are not the only kinds, they are probably the most widely distributed. It is unfortunate that none of these ants have common names except the *Attas* which are

Here we see a Trachymyrmex *worker cutting a small disc from an oak leaf. Note that the ant is standing on the disc which is being cut out. Often, the ant falls with the leaf fragment when it is severed.*

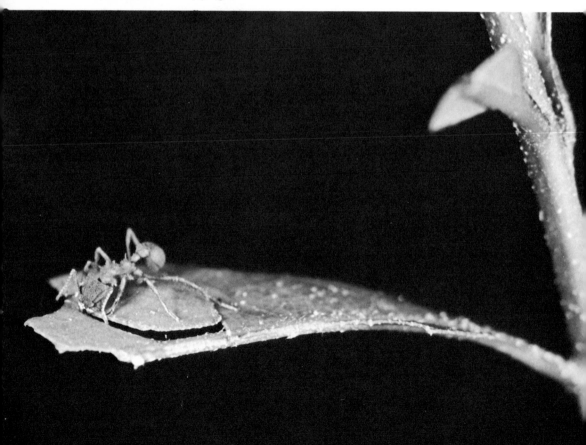

Trachymyrmex ants will live and cultivate their fungus in a glass container. This is such a nest with the honeycombed fungus garden at the center. In order to grow this fungus, the ants were supplied with bits of flower petals.

usually called leaf-cutters or town ants in the United States and *saubas* in South America. Other, lesser known, fungus-growing ants found here in our own country include the following:

Cyphomyrmex: Small ants which establish nests under bark, in rotten wood or in the ground. They range across southern United States and use vegetable matter and caterpillar droppings as a compost upon which to grow their fungus gardens.

Mycetosoritis: The habits of these ants are similar to those of the *Attas* but on a smaller scale. They are found in Louisiana and Texas.

Moellerius: Like the *Attas*, these ants gather leaves upon which to cultivate fungi. They occur in our Southwest.

It is a strange fact that the ants which cultivate fungi for food are all closely related, and are native to North and South America and the West Indies. In Africa and a few other places, however, there are termites which have developed somewhat similar habits. It should also be mentioned that, here in our own country, there are fungus-growing beetles known as ambrosia beetles (family, Scolytidae), which excavate tunnels in trees where they cultivate a special fungus upon which they and their larvae feed. But of all the insects that cultivate fungi, the fungus-growing ants are by far the most remarkable and interesting.

Chapter 7

The Honey Ants

ANYONE WHO HAS ever visited the arid deserts of Southwestern United States will agree that they are places where life for wild creatures is very difficult. Both the plants and the animals that dwell there must be specially fitted to survive the extremes of temperature and the uncertain rainfall. Noon temperatures near the ground may often exceed 130° F., while scant rains fall only at certain seasons. As a result, desert plants have developed methods of storing moisture. The cacti have eliminated their leaves, the work of food manufacture being taken over by thickened stems and twigs. Other desert plants, too, have adopted similar techniques in order to survive, as they have anywhere in the world where desert conditions prevail. On the deserts of South Africa, there are numerous plants that resemble cacti, although they are not really cacti at all but members of other plant families that have been changed to fit them to life in an inhospitable environment. Similar conditions prevail in the great desert regions of Arabia and Australia.

But it is not only the plants that the deserts have changed. Animals too have been forced to adopt special habits to enable them to survive there. Some of the most interesting of these adaptations are found among the ants that dwell on the sandy desert wastes. The honey ants, of which there are a number of kinds found in several parts of the world, have developed the habit of storing sweet honeydew gathered from aphids, mealybugs, plant galls, and plant nectar glands or nectaries. It is their method of food storage, however, that makes these ants of special interest. While they seem to be particularly fitted to desert life, it should be pointed out that not all kinds are confined to deserts; some kinds may occur in humid regions as well.

As a general rule, the honey ants, which have the habit of gathering

Other ants than true honey ants sometimes imbibe so much honeydew that their abdomens also become greatly swollen. Here are seen false honey ants (Prenolepis) feeding on sweet plant secretions. Notice their swollen abdomens. Sometimes they become so filled with honeydew that they have difficulty in walking.

large amounts of honeydew, belong to two ant subfamilies, the Camponotinae and the Dolicoderinae. These ants have thin abdominal walls, allowing them to become greatly distended with contained honeydew. While the abdomens of these ants often become swollen with honeydew, none of them ever imbibes sufficient honeydew to render itself helpless, as does the true honey ant to be discussed later. Among the more common of these so-called honey ants in eastern United States are the *Prenolepis* ants, small ants often observed crawling up the stems of plants or the trunks of trees. If a busy column of these little ants is closely observed, it can usually be seen that those individuals going up the stem or trunk have normal abdomens while those crawling downward have their abdomens swollen with contained honeydew. If one of these homeward-bound ants is observed against the sun, it can easily

111

Colonies of the true American honey ants (Myrmecocystus) *are common along the red sandy ridges of the Garden of the Gods in Colorado. These ants range from southern Idaho to Mexico City.*

be seen that its abdomen is swollen with amber fluid. The underground colonies of these ants are quite small, consisting of only about 300 workers. They are timid little ants that, in addition to their diet of honeydew, will also at times capture and eat small insects.

After returning to the nest, the *Prenolepis* workers regurgitate their loads to other workers or to their young. *Prenolepis* ants gather sweet honeydew and carry it home, but none of the workers ever take on the sole duty of serving as mere storage tanks for the colony's fluid food supply as do the true honey ants of the desert regions. In addition to the *Prenolepis* ants, there are several other ants found in various parts of the world that gather honeydew and carry it to their nests for immediate use. In no case, however, do any of the workers develop into living storage tanks.

Let us now turn our attention to the true honey ants *(Myrmecocystus)* of our dry, western deserts and desert-like areas. These are among the strangest of all ants. I shall not soon forget my first observations of these ants in their native habitat. I had traveled to Colorado to see and photograph them on the red, gravely ridges in the Garden of the Gods near Colorado Springs. This fantastic landscape lies beneath Pikes Peak, which towers more than 14,000 feet into the sky. It is a place where great, red sandstone figures of weird shapes rise from the ground and where shin oaks and other shrubs grow in profusion. My reason for choosing the Garden of the Gods as a place to study honey ants in their native habitat was based on a visit made nearly fifty years previously by the Reverend Henry C. McCook, a Presbyterian minister whose side line was the study of ants. Dr. McCook came to Colorado Springs in 1879. Actually, he was on his way to New Mexico where he had heard that honey ants were to be found, but while visiting a General Charles Adams at Manitou, which is really a suburb of Colorado Springs, he learned that the objects of his quest were to be found less than a mile away! It was fortunate that Dr. McCook stopped at Manitou since, as it turned out, it was an ideal spot to study honey ants. Previous to that time very little had been known about them.

For several months during the summer of 1879 Dr. McCook had camped in the Garden of the Gods and, from his description, I was able to locate almost exactly his original campsite which was located in a patch of woods just south of the junction of Adams and Von Hagen ridges. Nearby, I found the small mounds of red gravel and the entrances to honey ant colonies. Their nests may be confused with those of harvester ants, since both kinds occur there. Harvester ants are active during the daylight hours while honey ants are nocturnal. I was sure that I had found the tunnel to a honey ant nest when I saw the golden yellow guard ant in the entrance.

Since I did not wish to disturb the nests by excavation until I had had a chance to study their habits at night, I returned after supper. No ants were to be seen, but I was not concerned since Dr. McCook had found that their nightly forays do not begin until about 7:30 P.M. Now and then I turned on my flashlight but still no ants were in sight. Then, suddenly, they began streaming out of the nest entrance and crawling across the ground. Their destination was a nearby clump of shin oaks and when they reached these they climbed up trunks and out onto the twigs. Growing on these twigs were marble-sized galls, and it was these

The entrance to a honey ant nest is in the top of a small heap of gravel. The hole is quite large compared to the size of the ants.

galls that the ants visited. Minute droplets of honeydew were issuing from them, and these droplets were being collected by the ants. When the ants' abdomens had become so swollen that they could hardly walk, they hurried homeward across the gravely earth.

These oak galls have a strange story; they are produced on the oak twigs by a tiny wasp (*Holcaspis*) that lays its eggs in the tissues. Something secreted by the wasps' larvae causes the oak to produce the marble-sized galls. At night, a sweet substance called honeydew exudes from their surfaces and this is what the ants collect and carry home. At last, the ants seemed to have finished their work for the night and, one by one, all returned to their nest. It was nearly midnight.

The next day I returned to the Garden of the Gods and selected one of the colonies along the eastern edge of the ridge for excavation. It was located on the steep hillside and, I hoped, that by cutting away the hard gravel on the lower side, I would be able to focus my cameras into the exposed galleries. Little by little, I cut away the ground on the lower side of the nest. Progress was slow because of the flinty soil and the fact that I did not wish to disturb the ants by destroying their galleries.

114

At night the honey ants gather sweet honeydew which exudes from marble-like galls on the twigs of shin oaks. These galls are abnormal growths produced by a tiny wasp.

When the underground galleries are opened, the helpless replete ants with their greatly swollen abdomens can be seen suspended from the ceilings. Notice the two normal workers at the top.

After half an hour of diligent digging I at last broke into an opening. When I carefully enlarged it, I found myself gazing at an astonishing scene. Before me was a gallery with a more or less rounded ceiling. It was six inches wide and about two inches high and extended back into the hillside. But most interesting was the fact that, from the ceiling, were suspended numerous honey ants with their abdomens swollen to the size of small grapes. The abdomens of these individuals were so distended with contained sweets that the hard plates which had originally covered them now appeared to be mere islands on the globular surfaces. Each ant clung to the ceiling with its legs and made no attempt to escape or move. Indeed, after these individuals, called *repletes*, take on the duty of serving as honey tanks, they are almost completely helpless and never leave the nests again.

The morning sun, shining into the opened gallery, illuminated the repletes, causing their abdomens to glisten like glass marbles. A few of them had been dislodged from their perches on the ceiling and had fallen to the floor. Here they lay, waving their legs and antennae while their normal-sized sisters attempted to lift them up. The short fall had ruptured the thin membranes of some of the repletes' abdomens and the honey ran across the gallery floor. Worker ants began feeding upon it and this prompted me to sample some myself. I found it sweetish to the taste but not as good as the honey made by honeybees. Each replete contained almost half a teaspoon of the honeydew. Before the coming of the white man to America, the Indians often dug open the nests of these ants for the repletes, which were often eaten like candy. In Mexico, it is said that the natives extracted the contained honey and fermented it into an alcoholic drink. Dr. McCook estimated that about a thousand repletes would be required to make a pound of honey. The largest number of repletes he found in a colony was about six hundred.

The first gallery exposed was about a foot below the surface but there were other galleries both above and below this one. Each one contained repletes. Continuing careful excavations upward, I at last broke into a gallery located about two inches from the surface. This turned out to be the one where the pupal ants were kept. Each pupa was enclosed in a gray cocoon and, as is the habit of all ants, the workers scurried about attempting to save their young from harm. They

This is another view in a honey ant chamber, showing the golden abdomens of the repletes, or living honey tanks. At the extreme top is an ordinary worker with its jaws open in a threatening attitude.

A replete worker clinging from the ceiling of a chamber. Its abdomen is about the size of a small grape and golden-amber in color.

OPPOSITE: This close-up of a replete hanging from a chamber ceiling shows its abdomen so swollen with contained honeydew that the original plates are now mere islands on the globular surface. The white lines are a part of the ant's breathing or tracheal system.

Honey ant larvae spin cocoons before changing into the pupal stage. Here we see two workers carrying a cocoon, which is gray in color.

grasped the pupae in their jaws and carried them back into the dark recesses of the nest beyond view.

There are many things still unknown about these strange ants. Not the least of these is the manner by which the repletes are chosen for their life-long duty of serving as storage tanks. Once embarked on their careers as repletes there is no turning back; their greatly swollen abdomens make it impossible for them to leave the nest. Never again do they see the light of day. For years, perhaps, they hang from the ceilings of the underground passages. In summer they accept honeydew brought in by field workers, or dispense it to their hungry sisters. During autumn, when the oak galls no longer secrete honeydew, their store of food constitutes the colony's sole source of nourishment, and by spring their abdomens look like tiny deflated bladders. The repletes are the ants' answer to the problem of storing the liquid honeydew. Honeybees build waxen combs for honey storage, but ants do not have the ability to secrete wax, so they had to solve the problem in another way. It should be mentioned that, while honeydew from oak galls constitutes the honey ants' principal food, they also gather nectar from flowers and honeydew from aphids and mealybugs during summer. Sometimes they will also capture and eat small insects.

When a honey ant nest is excavated and the galleries occupied by the repletes are broken open, it is apparent that the normal-sized workers make every effort to protect them. These efforts are not very effective, however, since honey ants do not have stings and are not vicious biters. Nonetheless, they try and may be able to protect their honeydew "tanks" from invasion by other ants. It can be noticed, too, that the workers attempt to haul up the dislodged repletes and replace them on the gallery ceilings. In a few cases they are successful. Dr. McCook described how he observed a worker "dragging a rotund (replete) up the perpendicular face of a cutting made in the excavation of the nest. The mandibles of the two insects were interlocked and the worker backed up the steep wall, successfully drawing her protege." This was no small feat when one considers that the replete weighed about nine times as much as the normal ant.

Previous to Dr. McCook's detailed studies of honey ants, there had been a few observations made of them by various naturalists. Probably

120

the first person to record anything regarding them was Dr. Pablo de Llave of Mexico who published some notes on these unusual ants in a collection of *Memorias de Historia Literaturea Ciencias y Artes* in 1832. Unfortunately, Dr. de Llave's information was all second-hand, since he had never actually seen the ants himself, except as preserved specimens. Some of the information he gave regarding their life history was naturally not very accurate. As time passed, other observers made brief studies of these ants and they, too, made errors. For example, one naturalist stated that the repletes were actually a different species or kind of ant from the normal workers which, he said, were *black*. As stated previously, American honey ants are all golden yellow. Evidently, in excavating the honey ant nest, black ants from a nearby nest became mixed with the inhabitants of the honey ant colony and thus led him to a false conclusion.

This replete was photographed to show the translucent nature of its swollen abdomen. It is golden-amber in color.

It is now known that *Myrmecocystus* ants occur over a rather wide area, extending all the way from southern Idaho to beyond Mexico City. Usually, they are found along well-drained ridges in dry regions. As a general rule, their colonies are rather difficult to locate, since large mounds of excavated sand and gravel are not present around the entrances as is the case with harvester ants.

It is a strange fact that an ant in Australia has solved its liquid food storage problem in a manner almost identical to that used by the American ant. Here are two different ants living on opposite sides of the world that have arrived at similar solutions to a problem. Australian honey ants *(Camponotus inflatus)* dwell in the desert regions of the western portion of the continent where their colonies are found on the sandy plains among growths of mulga shrubs. Unlike their American cousins, they are black in color and, for this reason are often called "black honey ants." Apparently, their habits are similar and their repletes look almost identical to those of the American variety. These ants are considered to be a great delicacy by the Australian aborigines who most often dig many feet down through the hard soil to get them. To these sweet-starved natives, the repletes are known as *yarumpa* or *jirumba.*

Somewhat similar honey ants *(Plagiolepis trimeni)* occur in the desert areas of South Africa, a place where plants, too, have had to adopt special methods in order to survive. These African honey ants are yellowish in color and the abdomens of the repletes do not become as greatly swollen as do those of either the American or Australian honey ants.

Thus have sweet-loving desert ants in widely separated parts of the world solved their food storage problem. Without some solution to this problem they could not live in places where food can be harvested only during short periods of the year.

Chapter 8

The Herdsmen

APHIDS OR PLANT LICE are small, usually wingless insects which feed upon plant juices by inserting their beaklike mouth parts deeply into the plants. The plant juice or sap which they siphon out is very watery, containing only small amounts of sugar and other nutrients. In order to exist on this weak diet, the aphids must suck out large amounts. The digestive systems of aphids are designed to concentrate the food materials from plant sap and to allow the excess fluid to pass on out of their bodies. This excess fluid contains some sugar and is, thus, sought by many sweet-loving insects, including bees, hornets, ants, and other insects. This sugary material is sometimes called "honeydew." Honeybees often harvest large quantities of honeydew and store it just as they do nectar from flowers, but this honeydew "honey" is inferior to the honey made from flower nectar.

Ants of many kinds also make a habit of feeding upon honeydew, which is often their main food item. This habit is found especially among the ant subfamilies Dolichoderinae and Formicinae. The primitive hunters (Ponerinae) and the warrior ants (Dorylinae) "turn up their noses" at such food; they are flesh-eaters.

If you find a colony of either plant lice or mealybugs on a plant, there is a good chance that you will also find that certain ants are guarding them and harvesting the honeydew they produce. Here we have an example of *symbiosis*, a situation in which two animals associate with each other to their mutual benefit. Aphids are very helpless creatures, with no means of defense whatever. The ants, which feed upon the honeydew the aphids produce, have powerful jaws and can drive off most enemies. Thus, each is benefited; the ants "milk" their aphid "cows" and protect them from enemies.

123

Mealybugs also siphon juices from plants and produce honeydew. These fire ants are guarding their mealybug flock.

OPPOSITE: *Plant lice or aphids suck juices from plants of many kinds. Excess sweet material, called honeydew, is excreted by them and is fed upon by ants.*

One spring afternoon I found a colony of aphids on a willow twig. A number of black ants were busily lapping up the honeydew when a ladybird beetle, arrayed in red, alighted beside the aphid colony. Without delay, it began feeding upon the helpless aphids—but not for long! A vicious black ant at once rushed at the beetle and drove it off. This was a striking demonstration of the way in which ants protect their livestock. Many aphids have become quite dependent upon certain ants and are never found without them. Probably the best example of

125

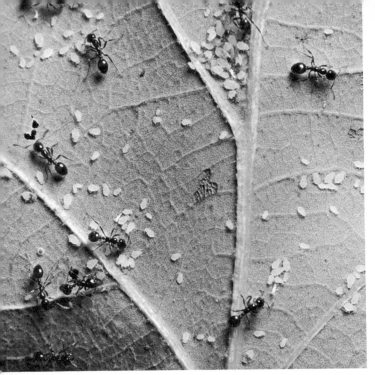

Ants also gather honeydew from aphids living on leaves. Here, fire ants guard their aphid "cows" on an oak leaf.

this is the case of the cornfield ant *(Lasius niger americanus)* which cares for the cornroot aphid *(Anuraphis maidiradicis)*, a serious pest of corn.

The seasonal history of these aphids associated with corn is as follows. During summer there are no male aphids; the females, generation after generation, give birth to living young through parthenogenesis. At the approach of autumn, however, male aphids are produced and, after mating, the females lay eggs. These eggs are collected by the ants and stored in their underground nests where they remain all winter, well cared for by the ant herdsmen, who transfer them from one part of their nests to another as conditions of temperature and moisture vary. With the coming of spring, the ants carry the aphid eggs out of their nests and place them on the roots of early weeds and grasses. When the eggs hatch, the young aphids at once begin sucking the sap from the roots and the ants feed upon the honeydew they secrete. At the end of about three weeks the aphids are full grown and begin bearing young. When corn begins growing, the aphids begin feeding upon its roots also, thus causing injury to the corn plant.

It is a strange fact that these aphids have been cared for by the ants for so long that they cannot get along without their help. Sometimes the winged aphids leave their underground feeding places and fly to new corn fields. After alighting, they seem helpless and would probably die unless picked up by a *Lasius* ant and placed on a plant root where they can insert their beaks and begin feeding. When these ants move their nests to new locations, they carry along not only their own young, but their aphid livestock as well. Like human dairymen, the ants go to great trouble to make sure that their "herds" are well cared for. Some kinds of ants that keep aphid livestock even go so far as to clip off their wings to keep them from flying away!

In addition to protecting their aphid "cattle," certain ants even build sheds for them! There is an acrobatic ant *(Crematogaster lineolata)* which constructs paper-like shelters of plant fibers around plant twigs to house and protect their aphid and mealybug livestock. (They are known as acrobatic ants from their habit of walking about with their abdomens held over their backs.) I have found and photographed the shelters of these ants on pine and other trees. Ants of other kinds also build such shelters.

Acrobatic ants (Cremato-gaster) of several kinds build shelters from plant fibers for their livestock. These are well constructed and have an entrance at one end. Notice the ant just entering the nest.

Fire ants sometimes construct "sheds" of plant debris over their plant lice or mealybugs.

When the "roof" of such a shelter is removed, the ants and their mealybugs can be seen.

An unusual aphid is one sometimes found in abundance on alder. This aphid (*Pemphigus tessellatus*) secretes long strands of white wax which hang down in strings. It also produces large quantities of honeydew which collect in golden globules among the waxy strands. Sometimes colonies of these are very large, completely covering alder limbs and twigs with their cottony masses. Such colonies attract large numbers of insects, all imbibing the abundant honeydew. On several occasions I have heard the buzzing of these insects from some distance away, even before I had seen the aphid clusters. Included among the visitors were honeybees, hornets, wasps, and large, black carpenter ants.

Least expected among the insects protected by ants for their sweet honeydew are the larvae or caterpillars of certain butterflies. These belong to the family Lycaenidae, and are sometimes known as little blue butterflies. Lycaenid caterpillars are of unusual form, being more or less sluglike. While most of them feed upon leaves, there are a few closely related caterpillars that actually devour aphids. The wanderer butterfly (*Feniseca tarquinius*), common in eastern United States, lives entirely on a diet of aphids. On the other hand, there are numerous plant-eating lycaenid caterpillars that have glands on their backs which secrete a type of sweet honeydew much relished by ants. These caterpillars, like aphids, are quite defenseless and so are protected by the ants in return for the honeydew they produce. The ants caress the little caterpillars with their antennae just as they do their aphid "cows," and the caterpillars respond by secreting droplets of honeydew. Some of these caterpillars actually live in ants' nests where they are protected. The tailor ants of the Tropics often keep these caterpillars in their silken nests, and it is said that the female butterflies always select trees inhabited by the ants in which to lay their eggs. The butterflies seem to know which kind of ant will protect their young and apparently select only those plants inhabited by them.

In India and China there grows a small tree known as Jerusalem thorn or Christ's thorn (*Zizyphus*). The caterpillars of a small blue butterfly (*Tarueus theophrastus*) feed upon the leaves and are attended by large black ants which usually nest at the base of the tree. During summer the ants protect the caterpillars and stroke them for the sweet substances they secrete. At the approach of autumn, when the cater-

129

pillars are full grown, the ants dig holes in the ground beneath the tree. Other ants then convoy or drive the caterpillars down the tree to the holes in which they transform into pupae. Thus, the ants seem to have the foresight to make sure that their caterpillars will be safely preserved beneath the ground and emerge in spring to lay more eggs to make more caterpillars.

Quite recently, an interesting case of ant-caterpillar association was discovered by Gary N. Ross in the Tuxtla Mountains of southern Mexico. The ants involved were Mexican carpenter ants *(Camponotus abdomoninalis)* which tunnel in wood. The caterpillars they guard for their sweet, honeylike secretions are a new species or kind of metal-

Cottony aphids live on alders, and secrete white, waxy material. They also produce golden droplets of honeydew which are fed upon by ants. This ant with her flock of aphids is the yellow carpenter ant (Camponotus).

mark butterfly named *Anatole rossi,* after their discoverer. During the daylight hours, the caterpillars are kept in earthen cavities or "pens" located at the bases of Croton plants. At the approach of dusk, the ants go up and explore all parts of the plants to make certain that no enemies are present. Assured that all is well, the caterpillars are then liberated from their "pens" and allowed to crawl up the stems to commence feeding on the leaves. Here they remain all night, feeding, and guarded at all times by the ants who, periodically, "milk" them for their sweet secretions. With the approach of dawn, the caterpillars are herded down the stems again and into the "pens" for the day. Once inside, the outside entrances are plugged to keep enemies out. Each day, the ants go through this same routine. Eventually, of course, the caterpillars become mature and change into the pupal or chrysalis stage. During this helpless period, also, they are protected by the ants, since they still have sweet-secreting glands. These chrysalids have tiny sound-making, or stridulating, organs, used perhaps to call their protecting ants. When the butterflies hatch out, they are allowed to fly away since the ants have no further interest in them. In a rather cruel little experiment, Mr. Ross placed a number of the caterpillars on a plant without their protective ants. He reported that all these caterpillars were captured by enemies within a few hours. Thus, it is obvious that without their ants, the caterpillars cannot long survive.

In the cases described above, the butterfly caterpillars are all more or less dependent upon their ants for protection. Thus, it is surprising to find that there is a lycaenid caterpillar in Europe *(Lycaena arion)* which, during most of its life, feeds upon plants. However, during the latter part of its life as a caterpillar it changes its food habits and enters a nest of *Myrmica* ants where it preys upon their young.

Chapter 9

The Slave-Makers

IT IS PERHAPS a strange and revealing fact that laziness is not confined to the human race, but is found among ants as well. Fortunately, King Solomon had never heard of these lazy ants when he advised the sluggard to consider the ant and her ways. It is probable that if he had known about these particular members of the ant tribe he would have chosen some other creature as a shining example of industry.

Just how the slave-makers' habit of enslaving other ants to do their work originated we have no way of knowing, but it is a fact that some queen ants take advantage of the "hospitality" of other ants in order to found their own queendoms. One of the common mound-building ants of eastern United States is *Formica exsectoides*, a species which constructs pyramid-shaped mounds as high as five feet. The mated queens of these ants are not content to fly away and endure the hardships of establishing colonies by themselves; this is too slow and uncertain. This queen locates a colony of the black *Formica* ant *(F. fusca)* and somehow gains entrance. Exactly how she does this is unknown, since most ants will kill any foreigner. In any case, she does get into the nest by some trick and eventually kills the rightful queen. This leaves the pirate queen in full charge of egg-laying. When her eggs hatch, they are cared for by the workers as if they were their own sisters. Eventually, of course, the original workers all die off and the pirate queen and her workers then have the nest to themselves.

In Africa there is an ant known as the decapitating or beheading ant, a name it well deserves. The queen of this ant colony, appropriately known as *Bothriomyrmex decapitans*, loiters near the entrance of a colony of *Tapinoma* ants. For some strange reason these ants are foolish enough to drag her inside. Why they do this we do not know, since

132

she is certainly a wolf in sheep's clothing if there ever was one. Within the nest, the brigand queen crawls upon the back of the rightful queen, where her foreign odor will not be noticed. In this position she is also able to carry out the next part of the drama. Using her jaws, she cuts off the rightful queen's head, an act that has earned for her the evil name of the decapitating ant! Strangely, the foolish workers then care for her and her young just as if they were caring for their own queen and her young. As in the case of the American *Formica* ant, the *Tapinoma* workers eventually die of old age and the brigand queen and her daughters have a ready-made nest.

There are many more examples of queen ants establishing colonies without the usual toil and uncertainties, but in each case, as Dr. Wheeler puts it, the ant nests preyed upon by pirate queens belong, as a rule, to "cowardly and prolific species." Among ants, at least, the meek do not inherit the earth; their colonies are destroyed by pirate queens.

From such acts of murder to actual slavery is but a short step. Probably the best known slave-making ants here in our own country are the blood-red slave-makers *(Formica sanguinea)* which enslave other *Formica* ants. The usual ant preyed upon is the black *Formica (F.*

An ant and its slave. At the left is the vicious red Formica *ant* (F. rufa) *and at the right is the black* Formica *ant* (F. fusca) *which it captures and enslaves to do its work. These black slave ants care for the red ants' young, feed them, sometimes carry their masters about, and even go with them on slave-hunting raids against their own kind.*

Ant-nappers at work. Slave-hunting Formica *ants plunder the nests of other species of* Formica *ants and carry off their pupae and larvae. When these young ants become adults they serve as slaves. When a nest is raided, the rightful owners make but little attempt at defense, often climbing up on grass stems while the slave-hunters go about their evil business.*

fusca). Instead of killing the queen, these ants raid the nest and carry off the helpless larvae and pupae. Thus, they are actually kidnappers. Such raids are made several times a year to maintain the large labor force needed to do the chores of the colony.

Scouts from the blood-red *Formica* colony roam the neighborhood looking for likely black *Formica* nests to raid. Once such a nest is located, the ants, bent on a slave-raiding expedition, leave the nest usually during the morning, though they may wait until late afternoon. Like army ants, they file out of the nest but, instead of narrow lines of march, they fan out as they move along. In watching these ants leave on a raiding expedition, it seems obvious that they know where they are going. The scouts, in some fashion, evidently afford leadership. Often the distance to the objective may be several hundred feet away and more than one nest may be raided on one trip out.

When the first raiders reach the nest they do not invade it at once, but, while awaiting reinforcements, surround it to make sure that the inhabitants do not escape. In the meantime, the black *Formica* workers attempt to save their young by carrying them up on grass blades or sticks. Soon the red kidnappers begin pouring into the nest entrances and shortly emerge carrying larvae and pupae in their jaws. The black

134

workers are not harmed unless they become too aggressive in the defense of their young. Apparently, it is a one-sided battle, since the black ants make but little effort to defend their home. In the meantime, the red *sanguinea* ants troop out of the nest carrying white larvae and pupae in their jaws. This is the booty of war. Usually, not all the larvae and pupae are stolen; a few are accidentally or purposely left and the inhabitants of the plundered *Formica* nest slowly set about repairing damage and again taking up life where it has been so rudely interrupted by the bandits. Colonies which have been plundered several times seem to develop a fatalistic attitude and thus offer little resistance to further attacks.

The young black *Formica fuscas* carried back to the nest face one of two fates; back in the red *sanguinea* nest it seems probable that many of them are eaten, while the rest are allowed to transform into adult ants. Evidence that many are consumed lies in the fact that not as many adult slave ants are found in a *sanguinea* nest as the number of young which have been captured. Thus, we are faced with the grim conclusion that a good many of the captured young are devoured by the warlike slave-raiders. It seems probable that the habit of keeping slaves may have originated from the *sanguinea* habit of raiding other *Formica* nests for young to be used as food. Charles Darwin believed that the slave-making habit originated as a sort of by-product of these raids. It could have happened like this: some of the captured young changed into adults before they could be eaten and become useful to the colony and so were "adopted." Thus, the slave-making habit gradually developed.

Blood-red slave-makers can get along without slaves if forced to. But while not entirely dependent upon slaves, they seem to derive much help from them. The black slave ants apparently aid in almost all the duties of the colonies, along with their captors. The red queens, however, are not capable of founding their own colonies. After her wedding flight the queen apparently does one of two things; she may obtain entry to another red ant colony and be adopted into it or she may enter the nest of a black *Formica* colony. Once in the black ant nest she steals a number of pupae and stands guard over them. If any of the black workers attempt to take them back she kills them with her

Red Formica *ants of the Rocky Mountains with a cocoon in the nest. This kind does not depend on slaves as do other* Formicas.

powerful jaws. She eats a few of the pupae to sustain her, but the re-mainder eventually change into adults and become her slaves. When she lays her eggs, these slaves care for and feed them. At some period during the early part of her stay in the black *Formica* nest she kills the queen and the situation is then well in hand, since she is the only egg-laying individual present. Eventually, the black slaves begin to die of old age and the red *Formicas* are forced to go out on slave-hunting raids.

While the red *Formicas*, as we have seen, can get along without their slaves, the amazon slave-makers *(Polyergus)* have gone so far in their dependence upon their slaves that they cannot live without them. Amazon ants are common here in our own country, being found in almost every state except, perhaps, those in the extreme South. They are called amazon ants from the Amazons of Greek mythology who were female warriors. The name is quite appropriate, since the workers, of course, are all females and are warriors of renown. Having been so long dependent upon their slaves, they have lost the ability to care for themselves and their young. Their jaws are sharp and sickle-like, perfect weapons for puncturing the body armor of enemies, but not of much use for carrying out household duties.

Like the red *Formicas*, they obtain their slaves by raiding black *Formica* nests. On these raids they are direct and aggressive and enter the *Formica* nests as if bent on serious business, which they are. Any ant foolish enough to oppose them is destroyed at once. Within the nest they pick up larvae and pupae and carry them back to their own nest where they are cared for by the slaves. There is great excitement in an amazon nest when a raid is about to begin. Even the slaves enter into the general furor and they accompany the amazon warriors on their raids. It is a strange fact that, even though the slave ants are timid when living in their own nest, after associating with the vicious amazons they tend to become aggressive like them.

Whereas only a few slaves are kept by the red *Formicas*, the amazons need a large number to do the work of the colony since they are helpless without them. As a general rule, from five to seven slaves are present for each amazon. These amazons truly live a life of luxury. At home in the nest, the slaves feed them and their young, excavate new nest chambers, and often carry their masters about.

The founding of new colonies by amazon queens follow, in general, the same pattern as that of red *Formica* queens. The mated queen finds a *Formica* colony, enters it, and eventually kills the queen and takes her place.

Thus goes the story of ants and their slaves. Of all the strange habits of ants, this is by far the most amazing.

Chapter 10

Ants and Their Trees

LIKE MANY BIRDS, a number of ants have taken to trees as places to live. In fact, this is where some of the most remarkable of all ants are to be found. While tree-living ants are especially common in tropical lands, some very interesting kinds occur here in our own country.

Not far from my home in Mississippi, there is a small grove of white ash trees. These trees are perfectly healthy and show no sign of insect damage, yet, within almost every twig, there lives a colony of ants. Known to science as *Colobopsis*, these ants are most unusual and worthy of anyone's study. I call them "trap-door" ants. Let us examine one of the white ash twigs. We see nothing unusual until we come to the mid-portion where there is a small hole about the size of the lead in a pencil. This hole has smooth edges and leads into the central pith zone of the twig. At first we see nothing but, if we watch quietly, the black hole seems suddenly to disappear! Closer examination shows that the head of an ant has been inserted into the hole from the inside, just as we would put a stopper into a bottle—except that it is inserted from the inside! The soldiers of these unusual ants have plug-shaped heads which they use like living doors to close the entrances to their tunnels in plant twigs. Strangely, when a person disturbs one of these ants it usually backs away from the hole it has been guarding, and only returns to its post after everything is quiet. It may thus seem that it is shirking its duty, but this habit does keep out small enemies who might try to enter the nest. I once kept some twigs containing colonies of these remarkable ants in my studio. One afternoon I placed an ant from one colony near the entrance hole to another colony that was plugged by an ant's head. The "foreign" ant tried to enter, but the soldier's head kept it out. She walked about the twig, returning to the entrance now

138

The round entrance to a Colobopsis nest in a twig. Notice the soldier's head plugging the entrance and a returning worker seeking admittance.

These trap-door ants live inside twigs. Here you can see the soldier's head and body as it blocks the entrance hole.

This close-up shows a soldier Colobopsis *ant in its tunnel in a twig. Note its plug-shaped head.*

and then to see if the "door" was open. It never was. She remained near the entrance for several days before becoming discouraged. This little experiment proves that "foreign" ants, even of the same kind, are not admitted to the nest. Evidently, they do not know the password or do not have the proper colony odor.

There is considerable evidence that ants identify themselves to the guards by means of touch. Dr. William Morton Wheeler states that returning workers are admitted "after gently knocking at the living portal with their delicate antennae." Dr. Wheeler tried to trick a guard ant by touching its head with a straw, but the ant was not fooled.

Colobopsis ants—there are several kinds—are native to southern United States from Texas eastward, but similar ants are found in Europe and some other countries. The various kinds are more or less selective in the places they nest; some kinds prefer white ash, others are found in sumac, and still others excavate tunnels in tree galls. They prefer the twigs and small limbs of trees having soft, inner pith which can easily be removed.

If we split open a twig containing a *Colobopsis* colony, we find that it contains twenty or more ants, most of which are of ordinary "ant" form but, among these, there are several plug-headed members of the soldier caste. The usual proportion of soldiers to workers is about one soldier to five or six workers. Usually, larvae and pupae are also present. If we examine one of the soldiers under a hand lens we find that its head is elongate and "flat-faced" and definitely resembles a bottle cork. When one of these soldiers is in position with its head closing the entrance hole, only the front of its head and the jaws are exposed to the outside. Both eyes and antennae are concealed. We might well speak of this ant as "the ant that uses its head."

Colobopsis ants live upon honeydew gathered from plant lice out on the leaves of the trees where their colonies are located. When a worker, bent on leaving the nest tunnel, approaches the entrance, the guard

In their tunnel in a twig are a Colobopsis *soldier (top) and a worker (below). Also present are larval ants.*

141

backs out of the hole, closing it again after the worker has gone. Upon her return, the worker identifies herself in some fashion to the guard, who backs away and admits her.

While "foreign" ants are usually denied admittance to a colony, there is evidently some "visiting" between colonies in twigs on the same tree. I once dusted the ants in a colony with a fluorescent powder and, a few days later, examined other colonies on the same tree under ultraviolet light, which makes the fluorescent powder glow. Some of the powder was found in every colony, proving that there had been considerable mingling of ants among the various colonies. How this occurs I am unable to explain, in view of the experiment I had previously made with the ant who was refused admittance to the "foreign" nest. The truth is, of course, that all the colonies in a tree are apt to be closely related, having usually been founded by queens produced by one original colony.

While many *Colobopsis* ants excavate their own tunnels in twigs and stems, others use any available cavity as a nesting place. In this respect, their habits resemble those of the carpenter ants *(Camponotus)*, to which they are closely related. In our Southwest, near the Mexican border and on down into the Tropics, there is found another ant *(Cryptocerus)* with habits similar to the *Colobopsis* ants. On the top of the soldiers' heads of these ants there are discs which fit into the oval entrances to the nest cavities, which are usually located in the dead twigs of trees and shrubs. Another group of twig-inhabiting ants is found in the West Indies, Central America, southern Texas, Arizona, and the Florida keys. These ants *(Macromischa)* do not have special adaptations for closing their nest entrances, but they do excavate tunnels in twigs and small limbs. They walk in a leisurely fashion and are reddish in color with black abdomens which are usually bent forward under their bodies as they walk about. They feed upon small insects

142

Head-on view of a Crypto-cerus ant, showing its pe-culiar head. These tropical ants are jet-black in color.

LEFT: *This is a tropical twig-inhabiting ant* (Macromischa). *It nests in holes in twigs and limbs and often walks about with its abdomen bent forward beneath its body. Some kinds of these ants occur in southern Florida.*

RIGHT: *These ants* (Azteca schimperi) *build paper nests in trees which resemble those constructed by hornets. They are found in the American Tropics.*

and plant nectar. The larvae of many twig-inhabiting ants have special adaptations to fit them for the unusual places in which they live. Some of these larvae have hooked hairs on their backs which probably keep them from falling in the hollow, vertical stems.

While the ants described above show the most remarkable adaptations to life within twigs, they are not the only ants that dwell there. If a number of stems, such as sumac and other shrub and tree limbs, are split open, some of them are apt to contain ant colonies of other kinds. One kind which commonly nests in such situations is the acrobatic ant (*Crematogaster*), though these interesting little ants may be found almost anywhere. Called "acrobatic" because of their habit of holding their triangular abdomens over their backs, these ants feed upon honeydew obtained from plant lice or aphids and mealybugs. One kind of acrobatic ant (*C. lineolata*) often goes to the trouble of constructing shelters or "barns" over its aphid or mealybug livestock. These shelters are built of plant fiber and resemble, in a general way, the type of building material used by hornets. These paper or carton shelters en-

144

circle twigs and have entrances at the ends. They may often be found on small pines but are also built on other trees. Another acrobatic ant (*C. atkinsoni*), which occurs in the Southeast, builds a somewhat larger carton nest on sedges or rushes, usually a foot or so above the ground. These paper nests may often be as large as a human head.

In Florida, the carton-building kinds of acrobatic ants are quite common. One kind (*C. clara*) builds nests in marsh grass (*Spartina*), usually a foot or so above the ground. These paper nests may be as large as twenty inches high and six inches in diameter, and are made of plant fiber and bits of leaves attached together.

It is in the Tropics, however, where most of the ants which build paper nests are most abundant. In Central and South America there are several kinds. One of these is the carton-building ant (*Azteca trigona*) which suspends its paper nest from tree limbs in a manner quite similar to that of our bald-faced hornets.

Some of the world's most unusual tree ants also occur in the Tropics. We now turn our attention to Costa Rica where, on the hillsides and sandy, coastal areas of this country and other Central American lands, as well as in Mexico, there grow low, spreading shrubs which are pro-

Bull-horn acacia trees are covered with stout thorns within which live small Pseudomyrma *ants. Notice the entrance holes made by the ants in some of the thorns. The presence of these stinging ants protects the trees from leaf-eating enemies. This photo was made near Veracruz, Mexico.*

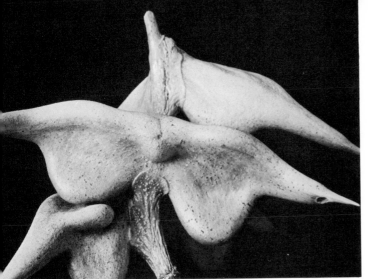

The thorns of a bull-horn acacia, with an ant entrance in one thorn. The ants make only one entrance hole in each pair of thorns.

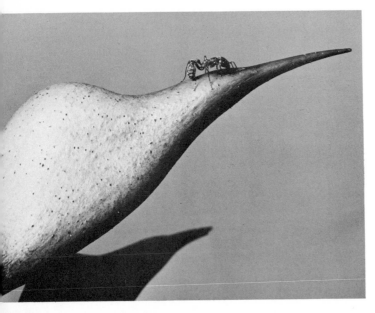

There are many different kinds of bull-horn acacias and their thorns vary in shape. This is an acacia thorn with a Pseudomyrma ant at the entrance to its nest.

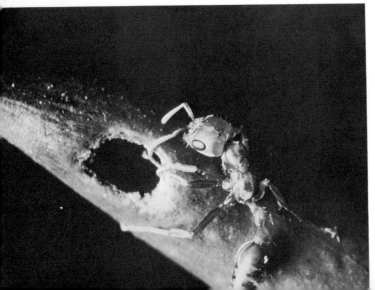

Here we see a Pseudomyrma ant at the entrance to its nest in a bull-horn acacia thorn. These slender ants are very alert and active.

A view of an acacia thorn cut open to show the ant colony inside. Within this cavity are larvae of various sizes and several pupae.

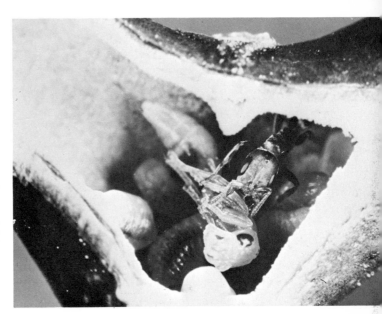

When this acacia thorn was cut open, a worker Pseudomyrma ant attempted to pull a pupa back to safety. In the background are larvae.

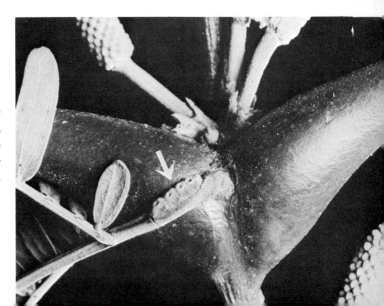

Here is a close-up of the nectary craters (arrow) at the base of an acacia leaf near its attachment to the thorns. Within these craters is produced the honeydew upon which Pseudomyrma ants feed.

tected by numerous large, sharp spines that look rather like bulls' horns. Their leaves resemble those of mimosa, in that they are divided into many small leaflets. Because of the shape of the thorns, these shrubs or low trees are known as bull-horn acacias. To the early Mexican Indians, they were known as *Hoitzmamaxalli* trees. In truth, there are nearly thirty different kinds of bull-horn acacias growing in various localities, but they are all rather similar and belong to the pea family.

Our knowledge of these acacias goes back to the year 1570 when King Philip II of Spain sent Francisco Hernandez to the New World to obtain information on its natural resources. In northern Mexico, along the Pànuco River, Hernandez discovered some unusual trees of which he wrote as follows:

"The Hoitzmamaxalli is a tree with leaves resembling those of a mezquite or tamarind, yellow flowers, edible pods, and horns very like those of a bull, growing upon the tree's trunk and branches . . . Moreover, within the horns there are generated certain slender ants, tawny-colored and blackish, whose sting is very hurtful."

Señor Hernandez was a most careful observer, but he missed the most important point in regard to the ants, since these ants *(Pseudomyrma)*, which make their homes within the thorns, have a remarkable relationship to the acacia trees.

Before maturity, the large thorns are filled with pith and covered by hard, outer walls. When mature, the ants gnaw an entrance hole into one of each pair of thorns and remove all the soft pith. The entrance is made near one of the tips. Within the paired thorns, the ants establish their colony and begin rearing young, well protected by the hard shell-like walls. It would seem as if the tree had purposely provided these slender little ants with a safe home and, apparently, this is true, since the ants pay their rent by protecting the leaves from leaf-eating insects, especially leaf-cutting ants which are able to defoliate a tree in one night. But not only does the acacia provide snug homes for its standing army of *Pseudomyrma* ants; it also furnishes food for them. At the base of each leaflet-bearing twig, there is a row of crater-like glands which secrete a honey-like liquid upon which the ants feed. But this is not the whole story; if the ants had only to visit the conveniently

148

placed honey glands for their nourishment they would not go out on the leaves, which might be destroyed by leaf-cutting ants or leaf-eating beetles. So, in order to make sure that the *Pseudomyrma* ants will be continually out patrolling its tender leaves, the acacia uses another trick. It produces, at the tip of each leaflet, a fruitlike body which is reddish in color and relished by the ants. These are gathered by the ants and carried back to their nests, but while out on their harvesting forays the ants are also present to repel leaf-eating enemies of the tree. Here we have what is probably the world's most remarkable example of plant-insect cooperation. Many millions of years of evolution and adaptation must have been required to perfect it. The ants have food and lodging, and the acacia, in return, receives protection from enemies.

The first naturalist to study these ants and their acacias was Thomas Belt, who recorded his observations in his book, *The Naturalist in Nicaragua*, published in 1874. Since Belt discovered the relationship between the acacia and its ants, the fruitlike bodies at the tips of the leaflets are known as "Beltian bodies." Attention should be called to the fact that these nutritious bodies have no relationship to seeds or true fruit; they are apparently produced on the leaves for the sole purpose of enticing the ants.

While bull-horn acacias are natives of tropical lands from Mexico southward, they are also grown in southern Florida. A gentleman in Fort Meyers has almost every known species growing in his garden. They bloom and produce seeds just as in their native lands, even though their protective ants are absent. It should be remembered, however, that in Florida, there are no leaf-cutting ants.

That the *Pseudomyrma* ants, which live within the thorns of the acacias in their native lands, form an effective police force there can be no doubt. The ants are slender, very alert and active, and bite and sting viciously. In the United States there are found some small ants *(Leptalea)* which are very closely related to the bull-horn acacia ants, but these ants nest in grass stems and in the twigs and branches of trees.

Another very unusual example of tree-ant association is that of cecropia trees and *Azteca* ants *(A. muelleri)*, but we must again travel to the American Tropics to study them. Cecropia trees, which grow only in warm countries, often attain a height of thirty feet. Their leaves are

This kind of acacia grows in Nicaragua. Seen here are the Beltian bodies (arrow) at the tips of the leaflets which the Pseudomyrma ants harvest and carry back to their nests in the thorns. Additional Beltian bodies are seen on leaflets near the bottom of the picture. These edible "fruits" entice the ants out to the leaves where they will be present to drive off leaf-eating enemies.

Close-up of a winged queen Pseudomyrma ant on an acacia thorn in Costa Rica.

large and have several lobes resembling those of the castor bean. When dry, they curl up into attractive forms of silvery color and are often used for decorative purposes.

Cecropia trees belong to the mulberry family and have a milky juice. Their branches are few in number and widely spaced, with the lowest one usually arising many feet above the ground. Probably the most interesting thing about the cecropia tree, however, is its hospitable nature; it seems to attract many inhabitants who live upon and within it. Sluggish tree sloths creep among its branches and feed upon its leaves, as do howling monkeys. Various birds feed upon its catkin-like blooms. But of all the varied inhabitants of the cecropia tree, none are more abundant or amazing than the small *Azteca* ants which dwell within the hollow passages of its trunk and limbs. Probably this tree's most unusual feature is the fact that its trunk and branches are hollow with many cross-walls, or *septa*, like the stems of the bamboo. Because of these hollow spaces, the cecropia is peculiarly suited to the *Azteca* ants. While some kinds of *Azteca* ants build paper nests, which they suspend from tree limbs, the cecropia ant lives within the hollow cecropia tree as if it were an ant apartment house. The nest proper is

A cut-away view of a cecropia tree. Ants (Azteca muelleri) build their paper nests within the hollow trunks of cecropias, and also cut holes through the cross-walls in the trunks and limbs so they will have passages to all parts of the trees. The close-up of the growing tip of a branch shows the exit holes (see arrows) made by the ants and structures at the bases of the leaves which contain the small müllerian bodies upon which the ants feed. The presence of these ants keeps leaf-eating enemies away from the cecropia tree.

located in the main trunk of the tree a short distance above the ground and is built of paper. In this respect it resembles the nests constructed by those *Aztecas* which suspend their nests from limbs. In building the oblong nest, the ants cut away the inner walls of the trunk so that they are thinner than normal. Due to the weight of the tree, the walls gradually bend outward, causing a bulge in the trunk when viewed from the outside.

Within the tree, the ants gnaw holes through the various cross-walls of the trunk and limbs so that they can travel from the nest in the trunk to all parts of the tree from the inside. Here and there, small entrance holes are made to allow them to visit the foliage and other outside portions of the tree. Thus, the ants have a perfect, made-to-order apartment house where they can live secure from most enemies. But, like the bull-horn acacia trees, the cecropia receives some benefit in return. Again, like the acacia, the cecropia is often attacked by leaf-cutting *Atta* ants which destroy its leaves. When the *Attas* invade the tree, the cecropia ants rush out and attack them with their jaws. Unlike the *Pseudomyrma* ants which live in the thorns of the bull-horn acacia, the *Azteca* ants have no stings. Cecropia trees that harbor colonies of *Azteca* ants—and most of them do—are rarely visited by leaf-eating insects, especially *Attas*. In return for this police service, the cecropia produces food for its ants, just as does the bull-horn acacia. In this case, the tree produces small fruit bodies in hairy cushions at the bases of its leaves. These are called müllerian bodies and are eaten by the *Azteca* ants. Thus, apparently both the cecropia ants and their trees are benefited, but not all naturalists agree. One early student of these ants and their trees stated that the cecropia needed its protective ants "like a dog needs fleas"! It is true that a cecropia may live without its ants, but most authorities believe that the tree is benefited by them. It is also true, though strange, that when the cecropia dies, the ant colony within its trunk dies also.

Most of us tend to think that strange things are found only in far-off places. Thus, it may come as a surprise to you to learn that, here in our own country, there are native plants that entice ants for the protection they give against leaf-eating enemies. Many plants, including castor bean, elder, partridge pea, and others, possess nectar glands, or nec-

152

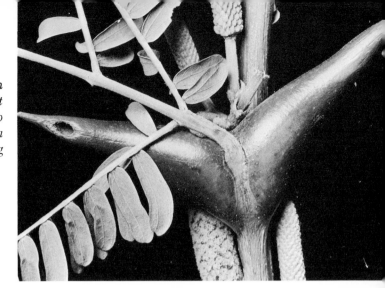

Close-up of a pair of bull-horn acacia thorns showing the ant entrance made in one thorn. Also seen in this picture are the acacia leaves and yellow flowering heads.

Some of our native plants have nectar glands which attract ants for the protection they afford against leaf-eating insects. Shown here is an ant feeding at a nectary on a partridge pea.

This picture shows a golden globule of nectar upon the nectar gland of a partridge pea leaf stem.

taries, which are regularly visited by ants. It is probable that the presence of these ants discourages attack by beetles and caterpillars. In no case, however, does any plant or tree in our country provide both food and living quarters for its protective ants as do the bull-horn acacias and the cecropia trees in the Tropics.

One might suppose that the *Azteca* ants, living within the cecropia tree, would be safe except that they do have some enemies. One of these is the large pileated woodpecker, characterized by its black color and flame-red crest, which chisels holes into the cecropia trunk and branches and captures the ants. Where cecropia trees inhabited by *Azteca* ants are abundant, these ants are the chief item in the diet of the pileated woodpecker.

On the island of Guam, I was once walking down a jungle trail and noticed a ball-like mass in the fork of a small tree. At first I thought it was a bird's nest but, upon closer examination, I found that it was an "ant garden." It consisted of earth and vegetable material held together by the roots of many tiny plants that were growing on it. Within this sphere, which was about the size of an orange, were the tunnels of an ant colony. Unfortunately, I had no container in which to collect any of the ants and so do not know what kind they were. Many years ago, such ant gardens in the deep forests of the Amazon were found to be inhabited by certain species of *Azteca* ants (*A. olithrix, ulei,* and *traili*) as well as by one of the carpenter ants (*Camponotus femoratus*). The discoverer of these ant gardens believed that the little plants growing in them were from seeds planted by the ants, since he saw them carrying seeds. It seems more likely, however, that the plants which grow in these "hanging" gardens result from wind-blown seeds. Thus, the presence of the plants is more or less accidental.

While it would be difficult to decide which of the world's many tree-inhabiting ants is the most interesting, the weaver ants would certainly be among the candidates for first choice. These ants are found only in certain tropical lands, especially the East Indies and Australia, although one weaver ant also occurs in Brazil. The weaver ants found in Ceylon and nearby areas belong to two closely related genera or groups (*Oecophylla* and *Polyrhachis*). They build nests by attaching tree leaves together with silk, thus forming snug, waterproof structures. They live

154

This is one of the weaver or tailor ants (Polyrhachis) *which uses its larvae like bobbins as sources of silk to "sew" leaves together to form nests. This one is from Borneo.*

among green leaves, and some kinds are green in color, a most uncommon hue among ants. Actually, there is nothing very unusual about the nests which these ants build, but their method of construction is remarkable, indeed. The leaves, as we have said, are attached together with silk, but no adult ant has the ability to secrete this useful substance. On the other hand, the larvae of many ants spin silken cocoons just as do caterpillars, but they all lose this ability when they transform into the adult stage. How, then, can these ants "sew" leaves together with silk? This remained a mystery for a long while, but eventually it was solved.

The best way to see how these ants work is to tear an opening in one of their nests and then watch them. The ants immediately swarm out and go to work repairing the damage. Some of the workers grasp the edges of the leaves in their jaws and pull them together. In the meantime, other workers rush into the nest and emerge with larval ants

155

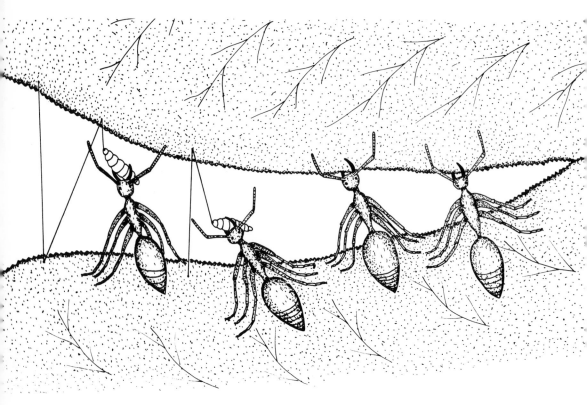

This drawing shows four tailor ants (Oecophylla) fastening leaves together. While two of the ants tug at the edges of the leaves, two others use larvae held in their jaws to "sew" the leaves together. As the larvae are moved from one leaf to the other, silk issues from their mouths. These ants are found in Africa and other tropical areas.

grasped in their jaws. While the first workers tug the leaf edges together, the other ants use the spindle-shaped larvae like bobbins. They apply the heads of the larvae to a leaf edge and the larvae obligingly begin secreting silk. As the larvae are moved from one leaf to the other, strands of silk issue from their mouths, gradually "sewing" the leaves together! When a "bobbin" is emptied of its silk, the worker ant goes into the nest and obtains another and the repair work goes on.

A German named F. Doflein (1905) was one of the early naturalists who studied these amazing ants. He says, "The soft and tiny grubs are held by the larger ants, who slowly move up against those pulling. Each grub is held by the middle, with head pointing forward, its snout

156

is gently made to touch the edges of the leaves where they are joined, it is slowly moved backwards and forwards and is undoubtedly issuing a thread during the operation, which adheres to the leaf edges, and eventually grows into a web. When this web is completed it must be composed of several layers to be strong enough for the purpose of securing the leaves. . . . There could be no doubt that the ants were actually using their larvae both as spools and shuttles . . . with their mandibles they held their larvae so tightly that the bodies of the latter appeared to be compressed in the middle. Perhaps this pressure is necessary in order to excite the function of the spinning glands."

Here we have one of Nature's most remarkable examples of the way in which a problem is solved. The worker ant cannot secrete silk, so it uses its larvae which can. Here, perhaps, we have the world's first instance of "child labor"!

Chapter 11

Guests and Fifth Columnists

THERE IS AN OLD SAYING that "if you hang out the gourds the martins will come," which is just another way of saying that if you have extra room you will soon have guests. Long ago, when ants took up life in permanent nests where food and shelter were available, many "star boarders" moved in with them. The same thing probably happened when our remote ancestors began living in caves. Mice and rats found that, by living with humans, they were certain of an abundant supply of food. These small animals are still with us, in spite of the traps and poisons with which we attempt to destroy them. As time passed, our ancestors adopted and domesticated cats and dogs and these, too, have remained with us. Just so, many insects have been "adopted" by ants, with which they live almost in the same way we keep pets. There is, of course, a vast difference; the "pets" kept by ants originally moved in with them and were eventually accepted. Our ancestors, by contrast, captured and domesticated animals. Still, as we shall see, there is some justification in considering as pets some of the small insects that live with ants.

On the other hand, many of these insects are parasitic in their habits; that is, their presence is harmful to their hosts. The word "parasite" comes from a Latin word meaning "to eat at the table of another," and this is just what most ant "guests" do. While some of these guests devour food brought in by their hosts, other kinds are scavengers which live upon the waste materials found in the nests. Biologists call these *myrmecophiles*, a term meaning "ant-loving." This of course, is stretching the truth a great deal since they have no affection or love for the ants; they have merely found a safe place in which to live and feed.

158

My first experience with myrmecophiles occurred many years ago while I was studying fire ants *(Solenopsis)*. One day, while digging into one of the nests, I noticed a tiny, very active insect hopping about among the ants. I was able to capture it in a glass vial and, later, to examine it under a lens. I was astonished to find that it was a very tiny cricket with large jumping legs and no wings. These crickets, classified *Myrmecophila*, are rather common in ant nests of various kinds. They are the smallest of all crickets and occur in nearly all parts of the world. Usually, they are found associated with ants of certain kinds but, seemingly, each kind of cricket can adapt itself to life with several kinds of ants. One kind *(Myrmecophila nebrascensis)* may be found in the nests of such ants as *Formica, Pogonomyrmex* (harvester ant), *Camponotus* (carpenter ant), and others. These little crickets vary in size, but the larger kinds seem to associate themselves with larger ants. I have collected the kind found in the nests of the large, black carpenter ant *(Camponotus herculeanus pennsylvanicus)*. This cricket *(M. pergandei)* looks almost exactly like the one found in fire ant nests but is much larger in size, in keeping with the size of its hosts.

Now, as you might suspect, these minute crickets live in dangerous

Guest crickets live with various kinds of ants but they tend to vary in size with the size of their hosts. This cricket (Myrmecophila) *lives with large carpenter ants and is larger than the ones that live with the smaller fire ants and harvester ants.*

Shown here is a harvester ant and its small cricket guest. These tiny crickets nibble oily secretions from the legs and bodies of their hosts. They have powerful hind legs which enable them to jump away from the ants' jaws.

territory. At any instant they could be killed and devoured by their vicious hosts. Certainly this often occurs, especially if one of them is injured. The only thing that enables the crickets to survive is their muscular hind legs by which they can jump away from the slashing jaws of the ants. Now and then the ants snap at them like dogs snapping at fleas but, in general, they are tolerated or ignored. In addition to their own agility, the crickets have another thing in their favor; the ants cannot bend their heads around to reach them as they nibble at their hind legs, and the crickets apparently live by licking the oily secretions from the ants' bodies. This might seem very dangerous, but the crickets seem to have sense enough to remain as far from the ants' heads as possible. The relationship between the cricket and the ant may be more or less compared to that of the tick birds to the rhinoceros. The rhino pays no attention to the birds picking ticks from its back until they become too numerous; then it makes an effort to drive them off. In a similar way, the ants eventually become irritated by the crickets' nibbling and licking, and snap their jaws at them. To the crickets, however, this is merely an occupational hazard and they go off seeking other ants to lick.

While studying leaf-cutting ants *(Atta)*, I became acquainted with

160

an interesting little cockroach which lives in their underground fungus gardens. This cockroach (*Attaphila fungicola*) is one of the few "guests" known to live with the leaf-cutters, which seems strange when the abundant supply of food present in the nests is considered. The scientific name, *Attaphila*, means "*Atta*-loving," but, here again, it is the food and shelter which attract these guests. The little cockroaches are less than one-eighth inch long and are wingless. For some strange reason, their antennae are always clipped off short. Whether this is done accidentally by the small worker ants as they toil in the fungus garden or by the larger workers is unknown. The joints remaining on the antennae vary from seven to eleven, and sometimes more joints have been cut from one antennae than the other. Perhaps the ants purposely "dehorn" their "livestock"!

These roaches seem to dwell happily in the ant nests and often ride about upon the bodies of the larger worker ants, who seem to have no

Ants of many kinds have "guests" that live with them and share their food and shelter. Such a guest is a tiny cockroach (Attaphila fungicola) which dwells happily in the underground nests of leaf-cutting ants where it apparently eats the fungus cultivated by the ants. Notice that the little cockroach's antennae have been clipped off by the ants.

objection. In fact, these guests are almost completely ignored by their hosts. They live in the fungus gardens like mice in our cellars, but apparently are never abundant enough to cause harm. They feed upon the fungus as do their hosts and, in general, seem to lead carefree lives.

The close association between the diminutive roaches and the ants is probably a very ancient one. Since they live in darkness as complete as that in a cave, they have little use for eyes. As a result, their eyes have become greatly reduced in size and, whereas each compound eye of a common cockroach is made up of about eighteen hundred individual "eyes," the eye of the guest roach contains only about seventy individual "eyes." Within the dark underground ant chambers there is, of course, little need for wings, so these have disappeared also, except that, for some reason, the hind wings of the males are still present.

Since the female cockroaches have no wings, you might ask how they get into newly established leaf-cutting ant nests. This question puzzled the early students of these insects, but the mystery has now been solved. These guest roaches, as we have said, have the habit of riding on the backs of their hosts; thus it is only natural that they should crawl onto the backs of the new queens before they take off on their wedding flights. When the mated queens excavate tunnels in the earth to establish new colonies the roaches are there with them. Thus, they hitchhike rides on the backs of the queens and take up residence in the new nests they establish. These roaches are also sensitive to the odor trails laid down by the leaf-cutting ants and can follow these trails just as the ants do.

There are more than 3,000 kinds of "poor relatives" and hangers-on that have taken up residence in ant nests. More than one-third of these are beetles, but there are also flies, mites, spiders, and even a few crustacea, in addition to the crickets and cockroaches we have already met, that have become guests of ants. Many of these star boarders have lived in ant nests for so long that they have come to resemble their hosts. For example, there is a bug (family Miridae) which resembles quite closely the red and black *Formica* ants with which it lives. There are also a number of tiny rove beetles (family Staphylinidae) that mimic certain ants so closely that, without a hand lens, they could easily be mistaken for them. Some of the most interesting of these are those that

162

live and travel with the tropical driver and army ants on their hunting safaris. These camp followers take advantage of the kills made by their ant companions. Those that live with African driver ants *(Dorylus)* and tropical American army ants *(Eciton)* are quite similar, even though they live on opposite sides of the earth. Even the smaller editions of the *Eciton* ants found in southern United States have such guests. Since all these warrior ants are blind (except for the males) and depend upon touch and odor in recognizing their sister ants, it seems probable that it may have been relatively easy for these camp followers to infiltrate their ranks and fool them into accepting them.

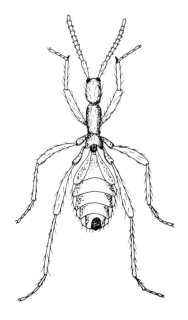

This rove beetle mimics Brazilian army ants with which it lives. Some of these ant guests look very much like their hosts.

Tropical army ants (Eciton) *have many guest insects which live with them and accompany them on raids. In the drawing below a strange wasp (left) masquerades as an army ant.*

In addition to insect myrmecophiles, there are several spiders which mimic warrior ants, not only in body form, but in their movements. These little spiders are "ant-waisted" like their hosts, and have even solved the problem of leg number. Spiders have eight legs while ants have only six, but these ant-loving spiders get around this minor problem by waving their forelegs about like antennae and walking on the remaining six legs like ants. Examples of such spiders are *Myrmarachne* and *Synemosyna.* There is also a rove beetle *(Dinarda)* that lives with the slave-making ants *(Formica sanguinea)* and when these ants go out on slave-hunting expeditions their rove beetle "pets" go along, following the procession like little dogs.

Some ant guests have been but little changed in form through long association with ants. The Hister beetles (family Histeridae) have very hard, seedlike bodies and many of them have taken up life with ants. In truth, the ants, in many cases, seem devoted to these little beetles

This immature bug (Megalotomus) *mimics an ant as it crawls about on plants, which probably gives it some protection from enemies. Other bugs also mimic ants. One of these is* Coquillettia mimetica, *a small plant bug which resembles ants very closely.*

and carry them about in their jaws. On the other hand, the beetles are very difficult for the ants to pick up; their hard bodies simply slip out of the ants' jaws. The relationships between these little beetles and their ant hosts are positively amazing as well as amusing. There is one kind (*Hetaerius brunneipennis*) which lives with *Formica* ants. These little red beetles are very agile and scurry about in the ant nest. The first part of their name, *Hetaerius*, is very appropriate, since it is of Greek origin meaning "friendship." They are very friendly with the ants. Now and then they sit up on their hind legs with their forelegs extended like "begging" dogs, and this is actually what they are doing. When an ant passes by, the beetle waves its forelegs to attract attention. Usually the ant stops and either tries to pick up the beetle in its jaws or begins licking it. Sometimes the ant can pick it up by one of its legs and carry it about. The body of the beetle apparently secretes a substance which the ant likes, so it licks it like a child licking a lollypop. Soon, however, the little beetle decides that the time has come for it to receive some food so it pushes its head out and opens its tiny jaws. The ant then obliges by opening her own mouth and regurgitating a droplet of food in the same manner as when feeding her larvae. Dr. W. M. Wheeler describes the antics of these ants and their little beetle "pets." He says: "Again and again the licking and feeding may alternate, as if the ant were fascinated with her pet and could not feed and fondle it enough . . . I have rarely witnessed a more comical sight than the behavior of these slender, black ants while they are holding the chunky, little red urchins in their paws and pouring liquid into them as if they were so many casks. Comical, too, is the behavior of the beetle while it is waiting to be noticed, with its head and forelegs elevated. At such times it assumes a ridiculous, cocky air. Often instead of receiving the caress and food it is expecting, it is inadvertently knocked over onto its flat back by some scurrying ant intent on more important business."

Not only do these Histerid beetles solicit food from passing ants, but they also feed upon dead ants or upon insects which the ants have brought home from hunting expeditions. While these beetle "pets" seem to be regarded by the ants with a considerable degree of what might, for lack of a better word, be called affection, there are other ant-loving beetles that dwell happily in ant nests and are almost com-

165

pletely ignored by their hosts. Perhaps they have been living with the ants for so long that the ants have simply gotten used to having them around.

Among the many myrmecophiles or ant-loving insects is found almost every type of relationship to their hosts that can be imagined. Many of them are thieves, pure and simple. One kind of thief is *Atelura*, a tiny silverfish insect which survives in ant nests only because of its agility and slick body. It gives its hosts nothing in return for its board and keep. It is the habit of most ants to regurgitate food to each other whenever they meet in the nest. *Atelura* takes advantage of this habit; when two ants are in the act of exchanging food it creeps up and steals a mouthful. Fortunately for *Atelura*, it can usually dash away in time to avoid the jaws of the ants.

The least expected of all the guests found living with ants are the caterpillars of certain moths and butterflies. In Brazil there is an ant (*Dolichoderus gibboso-analis*) which builds paper or carton nests in trees. The caterpillar of a small moth lives in these nests along with the ants, feeding upon the paper of which it is constructed. It also uses some of this paper to build itself a clamshell-like case within which it lives. When this little caterpillar has finished its growth and the moth is ready to emerge, it is covered with a dense growth of golden hairs. These hairs protect it from the ants until it is able to escape from the nest. In India and Australia, there is a little blue butterfly (*Liphyra*) which lays its eggs in weaver ant nests. Its larvae or caterpillars live in the ant nest and when the adult butterfly emerges, it, like the moth, is covered with protective hairs and scales. Any ant which attempts to attack one of the little butterflies becomes so entangled in the mass of scales that it quickly looses interest in the fray.

Another of the unusual inhabitants of ant nests is the larval stage of a Syrphid fly *(Microdon)*. These larvae resemble snail-like slugs and have often been confused with them. They have tough skins and creep slowly about in the outer passages of *Formica* and other ant nests. In the mountains of Montana I have found these larvae to be very abundant in these ant hills, and I have also seen the adult flies buzzing about over the ant hills waiting for a chance to lay their eggs. What these fly larvae feed upon in the ant nests is unknown.

While the beetles and other insects mentioned above all live happily in ant nests and, seemingly, are there by choice, there are other beetles, such as a small scarab *(Cremastochilus)*, that appear to be held in captivity by ants. If one of these little beetles attempts to leave, the ants carry it back into their nest. The beetles apparently secrete some substance that the ants find attractive and so are kept by the ants for that reason.

There is a family of beetles *(Pselaphidae)* whose members almost all live with ants and are known as "ant-loving beetles." These beetles are all very tiny and stout-bodied, and have clublike antennae. It is from these antennae that they received their name, which means "I feel my

There is one family of tiny ant beetles (Pselaphidae) *whose members almost all live as guests in ant nests. Some kinds secrete substances to which the ants are attracted. This one, named* Fustiger, *was photographed from a museum specimen.*

In this drawing an ant-loving beetle (Atemeles) *begs food from its* Myrmica *ant host. A similar guest beetle* (Lomechusa) *has tufts of yellow hair along the side of its body which are licked by the ants for some substance which they relish. These beetles live happily with the ants and are fed along with their own young. They can communicate with the ants by means of their antennae just as ants do with each other. Sadly, the beetles often devour the young ants.*

way." On the backs of certain beetles *(Claviger)* there are small clumps of hairs. When the ants touch these hairs, nearby glands secrete a sweetish liquid which they greedily lap up. These "pets" are licked and fondled by their hosts and, in general, their reactions resemble those of cats in a bed of catnip. The desire of the ants for these beetle secretions might also be compared to human addiction to narcotic drugs. Even more remarkable is the fascination which ants have for small rove beetles called *Lomechusa* and *Atemeles*. Another, closely related kind of beetle is called *Xenodusa*, which is most appropriate since it is Greek meaning "strange guest." It lives with carpenter ants. These beetles are common in the nests of several North American ants, which turns out to be unfortunate for the ants. The ants treat them even better than they do their own young because of the attractive secretions found in tufts of yellowish hairs along the sides of their abdomens. The beetles have been living with the ants for so long that they seem not only to be regarded as normal guests, but are able to communicate with them by antennal signals, just as the ants communicate with each other. Not only do the ants encourage and protect these little beetles, but if the ant nest should be disturbed and the ants decide to move to another location, they carry the beetles with them, along with their young. No human family could be more solicitous of its favorite cats and dogs.

Unfortunately, the presence of these beetles often has tragic consequences for the ant colony. The ants rear the beetle larvae along with their own, feeding and caring for them. Just before the beetle larvae are ready to pupate they are imbedded in the earth, along with their own young. Here the ant larvae spin thick cocoons, while the beetle larvae spin very thin ones. A large percentage of the beetle larvae are dug up by the ants, an act which accidentally kills many of them. It is fortunate for the ants that so many of the larval beetles are destroyed in this way because this is the only thing that saves the ant colony, since these beetles are actually fifth columnists of a very dangerous type. In effect, they are "drug peddlers" whose secretions are so desired by the ants that they will feed and care for them in preference to their own young! As a result, the young ants do not receive the proper amount of food and so do not develop properly. Those larvae which would have developed into queens develop, instead, into individuals that are neither queens nor workers; they are pale freaks who serve the colony in no way. Not only do the ants feed the beetle larvae food that should go to their own young, but the larval beetles devour the young ants. Here, certainly, is one of the strangest of all relationships between ants and their "guests." Some kinds of these beetles live with only one kind of ant, while others seem to have adapted themselves to live with several kinds. *Lomechusa strumosa* lives with the slave-making ant *(Formica sanguinea)*, while *Atemeles* lives with ants of several other kinds. This latter beetle has a very unusual habit; in spring, it moves into *Formica* ant nests in order to have its young reared by them; then it migrates into *Myrmica* nests to spend the winter. We might perhaps compare the rearing of these evil beetles by ants to the case of the cowbird which lays its eggs in other birds' nests and leaves to them the responsibility of rearing its young instead of their own.

There are many mites and small insects which live in ant nests, some of which are actually parasitic on the bodies of the ants. The relationships between all these alien guests and their ant hosts are often quite

169

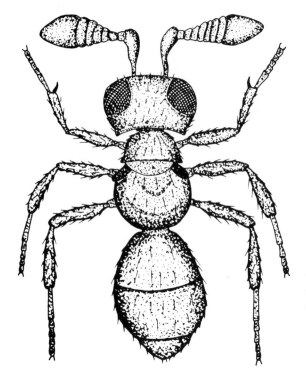

This strange little insect is actually a wingless chalcid wasp (Pheidoloxenus) *which lives with seed-gathering* (Pheidole) *ants. It is probably a parasite.*

complicated. We have seen how *Lomechusa* beetles live with ants to their sorrow, but these beetles, in turn, are often infested with parasitic mites. Sometimes *Dinarda*, another guest beetle which has been mentioned, eats these mites, thus benefiting the evil *Lomechusa!*

Even more dangerous than *Lomechusa* is a bug called *Ptilocerus*, found in Java. This "wolf in sheep's clothing" does not live in ants' nests but waits beside their trails. On the underside of this bug are found tufts of bright red hairs beneath which are located glands. If an ant, bent on business away from its nest, sees this bug, it is attracted by the red tuft of hairs. When it approaches, the bug rears up, exposing the red patch of hairs to the ant, who begins licking off the attractive secretion. Unfortunately for the ant, this secretion contains a poison which quickly paralyzes it. The bug then plunges its sharp beak into the ant and drains out its blood. *Ptiloceros* is, indeed, a highwayman to the ants which travel over trails through jungles of Java.

Chapter 12

Of War and Peace

AMONG ANTS as among men there are the "haves and the have-nots." Some ants live like wandering tribes, preying upon whatever game they can find. Others have taken up settled lives and live in communities. Still others engage in agricultural pursuits, harvesting seeds, or growing fungus food. Again, as in human societies, there are thieves and beggars among ants who take advantage of the industry of other kinds. *Smithistruma* ants are very tiny and live in small colonies, usually under stones or in decayed wood. Oftentimes their colonies are located close to the nests of other ants from whom they steal food.

The harvester ants *(Pogonomyrmex)* that live on the Great Plains construct high mounds beneath which their numerous tunnels are located. As we have seen, these ants gather and store plant seeds. With such an abundant store of food it is not surprising to find that thieves invade their nests. The tiny, yellow thief ant *(Solenopsis molesta)* often builds its small nest close beside the harvester nest and excavates little tunnels connecting with those of the harvesters. Thus, they have an easy means of entering the harvester brood chambers and devouring the young. Presumably, the large harvesters cannot enter the tiny tunnels of the thieves and so the thieves escape pursuit. Of course, if the harvesters "had sense enough," they could easily dig into the thief nest and destroy it, since they are much larger and more powerful. But for some reason they do not do this and so the thieves live happily with a nearby source of booty.

The harvesters are such easy "touches" that still another kind of ant also takes advantage of their hospitality. A small, vicious ant *(Dorymyrmex pyramicus)* builds its crater-like nests near the large harvester cones. These little ants are actually highwaymen, who hijack harvester

171

When flood waters invade ant colonies, some ants form themselves into balls which float about and finally touch dry land. This habit is found among leaf-cutting ants, driver ants, army ants, and many other kinds, especially in the Tropics.

ants laden with food they have gathered or captured in the surrounding area. Usually this is some small insect, since the harvesters often capture such insects to supplement their grain diet.

Another seed-eating ant *(Pheidole calens)* sometimes builds its nests near, or in, the cleared space surrounding harvester cones, and lives as a neighbor to its larger cousins. It is a nice arrangement, since the *Pheidole* ants can steal into the harvester nest now and then to make off with grain which these hard-working ants have stored in their bins.

All sorts of relationships are found among various ants. In Europe,

172

there is an ant which we might speak of as a star boarder ant *(Formicoxenus)*. This ant lives in complete harmony in nests of the red *Formica (F. rufa)* and, probably, eats its food. There is apparently no hostility between the two kinds of ants, and if the red *Formicas* should move to new quarters, their star boarders trail along, carrying their own young.

Another, slightly different, type of star boarder is often found in *Myrmica* nests in our northeastern states. This is sometimes called the shampoo ant *(Leptothorax emersoni)* since the workers, whenever possible, lick or "shampoo" the *Myrmica* workers. This, apparently, has two purposes; by their licking activities, they obtain oily secretions from their hosts' bodies, and their hosts often regurgitate food to them. Perhaps this is in return for the free shampoo!

Thus, we find that ants have a number of their lazy cousins living "within their gates." But these are not their only enemies, since small creatures of many other kinds have taken up residence in ant nests. These are in addition to those "guests" mentioned in the last chapter.

Ants are often infested with "lice" of several kinds, including mites, beetles, and flies. They also suffer from the attacks of internal parasites. Shown here is a uropod mite attached to a hair on the back of a fire ant (Solenopsis).

Mites of several kinds live like lice on ants' bodies. In Texas, there is found a fly *(Metopina)* whose larvae curl their bodies around the necks of certain larval ants *(Pachycondyla)* like fur pieces. When the ant larva is fed, the fly larva shares in the dinner. Strangely, the ants do not appear to resent the presence of these fly larvae.

One of the most vicious enemies of ants is another fly *(Apocephalus)* which lays its eggs on the heads of carpenter ants. When one of these eggs hatches, the larval fly enters the ant's head and feeds upon the tissues found there. Eventually, the ant's head falls off.

While afield on food-hunting safaris, ants also encounter many enemies. In the West, harvester ants are often waylaid by horned lizards (horned toads) which flick them up with their sticky tongues. Birds of many kinds eat ants as do frogs and toads. Woodpeckers drill into trees and capture wood-living ants of several kinds. In western mountains, the presence of bears is often revealed by rotten logs which they tear to pieces in their search for ants.

Among the more interesting ant enemies are ant-lions (insect family, Myrmeleontidae) which excavate tiny pits in dry sand or dust and trap them. The ant-lion is the larval stage of a winged insect which, in a

In Western United States, harvester ants on seed-gathering expeditions are often captured by horned lizards or "toads."

Ant-lions are the larval stages of dragonfly-like insects. They excavate small pits in sand and hide at the bottoms, where ants are trapped and devoured. At the right is an ant looking over the edge of an ant-lion pit. (See next photograph)

If an ant tumbles into an ant-lion pit, as has happened here, the ant-lion begins tossing sand into the air, making escape almost impossible. When the unfortunate ant slides to the bottom of the pit it is seized and eaten by the ant-lion.

general way, resembles a dragonfly. However, unlike the dragonfly, it is a very weak flyer.

When an ant-lion is ready to set its "trap," which is actually a pitfall, it backs around in a tight circle while tossing out sand. Eventually, a small pit about an inch deep is formed, having steeply sloping sides. The ant-lion then hides beneath the sand at the bottom of the pit and waits. It may wait but a few hours or it may wait for several days, but eventually some ant is apt to come along and investigate the pit. When this occurs, the hidden ant-lion begins tossing sand into the air with its jaws and the ant is apt to tumble into the pit where it is grasped in the ant-lion's needlelike jaws. These jaws are hollow, like hydermic needles, and at once a powerful poison is injected into the ant's body. This kills the ant and also slowly digests its body contents which are then siphoned out through the hollow jaws of the ant-lion. When the body of the ant is sucked dry it is tossed out of the pit and the ant-lion then settles down to await the arrival of another unsuspecting ant.

Another ant-trapper is the doodlebug, the larval stage of the tiger beetle (family Cicindelidae). These larvae, which may be more than an inch long, dig verticle holes in the ground and hide in them with only their heads and large jaws protruding. Like the ant-lion, a doodlebug may have to wait for a long while between meals, but eventually

Among other ant enemies are the larvae of tiger beetles which hide in holes with only their heads and jaws exposed. If an ant should walk too close, the tiger beetle larva or "doodlebug" reaches out and grabs it.

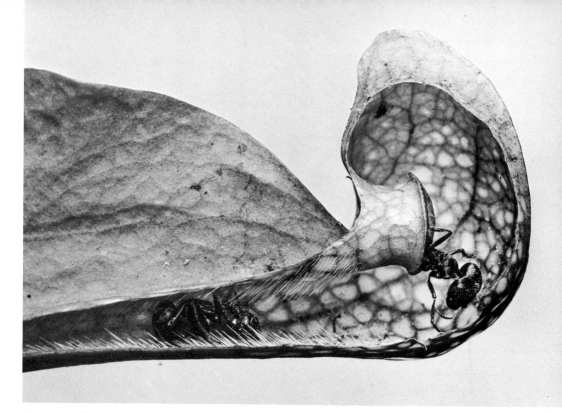

Ants are also captured by the leaf pitchers of pitcher plants. Shown here is a cut-away view of a pitcher plant leaf showing how ants are trapped. An ant enters the funnel-like opening into the spherical cavity at the right, attracted by some odor. Once in this cavity, it crawls deeper into the leaf (toward the left) where backward-directed hairs prevent it from escaping. Eventually, the ant is digested by enzymes secreted by the plant.

an ant comes walking along and the great jaws reach out and grab it. These insect larvae not only prey upon ants but will capture insects as large as a cricket. If a doodlebug should grab a bigger insect, it has an interesting mechanism to prevent its being pulled out of its tunnel. This consists of a series of hooks on its back which anchor it securely in its burrow.

Among the more unusual enemies of ants are pitcher plants (*Sarracenia*) which attract many insects into their tubelike leaves, where they are digested and their nutrients absorbed. I have often seen the leaves of these cannibal plants nearly filled with ant remains. The Venus-fly-trap (*Dionaea*) is another insect-eating plant found in the coastal areas of the Carolinas. Like pitcher plants, it often traps ants. The leaves of these plants are hinged like traps at their outer ends and have spines around their edges. These leaf traps, in the "set" position, are open

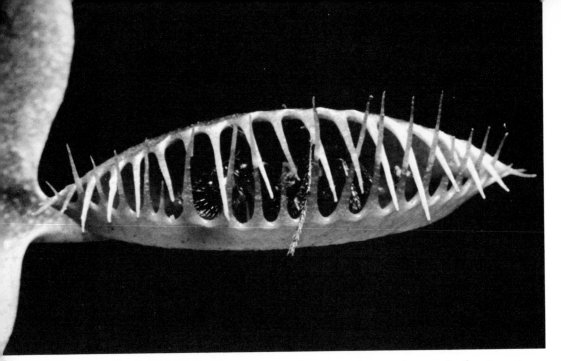

Among the unusual ant enemies is the Venus-flytrap. Ants and other insects are trapped by the leaves, which snap shut on them. Here is an ant imprisoned in a leaf trap of one of these plants.

wide and several trigger hairs are exposed on their inner, red surfaces. If a crawling insect such as an ant chances to crawl across one of these leaf traps, it is apt to touch these triggers, with the result that the trap snaps shut. In the closed position, the spines surrounding the edges of the leaf trap form a secure prison, effectively preventing the insect's escape. However, if such a wandering insect touches only one of the trigger hairs, nothing happens. At least two trigger hairs must be touched in quick succession to bring about the closing of the leaf trap. This trick has probably been evolved by the plant to prevent accidental closing.

Once the insect is imprisoned, digestive enzymes are secreted upon it from the inner surfaces of the leaf trap, and the insect is digested and absorbed. These plants grow in places where nitrogen is scarce and, since all animal bodies contain considerable nitrogen, the Venus-flytrap uses this means of supplementing the mineral elements it absorbs from the soil. This same thing is true of the pitcher plants and sundews. The latter plants use a different technique in trapping; their leaves are covered with glue-tipped tentacles which trap insects in the same way that flypaper does.

178

Ants in various parts of the world have enemies of many other types. In tropical countries there are anteaters that prey upon them, as well as upon white "ants" or termites. These creatures, of which there are several kinds, have greatly elongated tongues which they use to capture ants and other insects. The giant anteater (*Myrmecophaga*) of South America has powerful claws which it uses to open ant mounds, after which it inserts its long snout to capture the ants. This animal is about seven feet long. In Texas, Louisiana, Florida, and Mississippi there occurs a small relative of these creatures. This is the nine-banded armadillo (*Dasypus*), a small animal whose body is covered with horny plates. With its slender, piglike snout it roots in the earth, capturing ants and other insects. These strange animals, which may weigh up to fifteen pounds, are more or less nocturnal in habits and have very poor eyesight. They originally were found south of the Mexican border but are gradually spreading across all the southern states.

Perhaps the strangest of all the ant-eating animals is the aardvark, that creature so often encountered by people who work crossword puzzles. The name is of Dutch origin, meaning "ground pig." Its body is almost bare and its forefeet are fitted for digging into ant and termite nests. In addition to the aardvark, there are several other anteaters, including the scaly pangolin of Africa and Asia, the collared anteater, and the two-toed anteater which is about the size of a squirrel and has silky fur.

Anteaters prey on ants and termites, especially in tropical lands. To armadillos in southeastern United States, ants are tasty tidbits.

Chapter 13

Ants in Amber

THERE ARE MANY extensive forests in the world at present, but long ago even greater forests covered most of the dry land all the way from the Tropics to the Arctic Circle. At that time, the world's climates were warmer and, in addition to trees common to cool climates, many tropical trees grew as far north as Alaska and Siberia. These northern regions probably had climates rather similar to that of present-day Florida. This was during that period of ancient time known to geologists as the Oligocene Epoch, which began about 50 million years ago and lasted for perhaps 15 million years.

We read the story of this epoch in ancient rocks and stratas laid down by rushing streams that carried sediments down to lower areas where they buried plant and animal remains which slowly became fossilized. We know about the climates of that ancient world because of the kinds of plants that lived at that time and left their fossils, but we do not know why the world climates were warmer. In America, the Rocky Mountain chain had not yet risen high enough to prevent moisture-laden winds from carrying water from the Pacific Ocean eastward across the plains of the Midwest. These heavy rains, falling upon the ancient forests, carried mud and silt which accumulated in deep beds, furnishing clues to the rainfall of those long-gone days, while the fossilized plants and animals found in them tell us what kinds lived. There were colorful flowers which bloomed and were pollinated by flying insects. Ants of many kinds—some similar to modern ants—built nests and reared their young. In the streams and lakes, alligators lived as far northward as the Dakotas, and palms grew in Alaska.

Similar events took place across Europe and Asia. The great Alpine-Himalayan mountain system, extending all the way from Europe to

India, was in the process of rising, eventually to form the world's greatest mountains. In the forests which covered the land, there were many birds and mammals quite similar to those living today. In other places the land had sunk; the Sahara Desert, most of Brazil, and Panama were under the sea.

After these world-changing events, there came a time of quiet during which the great sub-tropical forests of the Oligocene period flourished. But there were places, such as western United States, where volcanic activity still occurred. Saber-toothed tigers roamed over the West, as did the ancestors of the horse.

In many places in the world, where semitropical forests occurred, there grew pinelike trees known to geologists as *Pinites succinifera*. For some reason or other, these trees exuded large amounts of resin. Why this was so we do not know; it is believed by some that it was caused by boring insects or, perhaps, by a disease. Some scientists, assuming that there *was* indeed such a disease, have named it *succinosis*. We can see such resin flowing out of pines and other conifers today, but this is usually caused by boring insects, especially beetles. The resin produced by trees serves as a protective agent, sealing up wounds and preventing the entrance of disease-causing bacteria and fungi. But modern pines do not produce resin in such vast quantities as did their remote ancestors which lived in the Oligocene forests. At any event, this resin was sticky and, like flypaper, trapped numerous insects and other things such as leaves, bits of wood, spiders, bird feathers, animal fur, flower parts, and microscopic pollen grains. After this resin had flowed from the living trees it slowly hardened into the transparent, plastic-like material called amber, which is usually dark yellow or brown. Eventually, this amber either broke off of the trees where it had been formed, or the trees died and decayed, leaving the amber in the soil. Naturally, not all the pieces of amber contained trapped objects, but a high percentage of them did. This amber, or fossil resin, is one of the best preservatives known to science. We still use a similar material, Canada balsam, to preserve specimens for microscopic study. It is composed of carbon, hydrogen, oxygen, and succinic acid. To geologists, amber is known as *succinite*. It can be ignited and burns with a smoky flame, and, for that reason, was known, in Germany, as *Burn-*

181

This is a photograph of resin flowing down a modern pine tree. Notice the ants (arrows) and spiders trapped in it. The ant at the top is a carpenter ant (Camponotus), while the one at the bottom is an acrobatic ant (Crematogaster). This is similar to the way in which ants were trapped in Baltic amber millions of years ago.

steyn or *Bernstein*, meaning "a stone which burns." Even more descriptive, perhaps, of the true nature of amber was its Latin name, *succinum*, meaning "sap stone," since it is actually the fossilized sap of a tree. On the other hand, the Greeks were interested in another characteristic of this strange material; they called it *elektron*. Since amber, when rubbed, acquires a charge of static electricity, the terms *electricity* and *electron* are derived from the old Greek word for it.

I have before me a piece of amber from the Baltic Sea. Within it are several insects and when I place it under a lens I can see that the insects are preserved in all their detail; I see their wings, their antennae, and eyes. It is difficult to believe that I am looking at insects that lived 50 million years ago; they look as if they had been trapped in the resin only yesterday. No other method would have kept them in such an excellent state of preservation. The ants, and other insects preserved in ancient amber, show all their minute external details, but their inner structure has disappeared. Insects' bodies are covered by a hard material called *chitin*, and this armor-like covering is the thing that made their remarkable preservation possible. The word *chitin*, by the way, comes from Greek and means "a coat of mail."

182

Since amber was once an important article of trade in all European countries, it had many names. In Finland it was known as *merrikiwi*, meaning "sea stone," from the fact that it was usually washed up on sea beaches. Our present word, amber, for this strange material was derived from the Arabic word *anbar* meaning "whale." Since amber is found on sea beaches, it was confused with *ambre gris*, or ambergris, a substance from whales much used as a base for perfumes. From the various names given to amber in various lands it is obvious that many people knew about it, as well as something concerning its origin. The ancient Greeks spoke of islands called the Elektrides (amber islands), but these were apparently imaginary. About the year A.D. 75, Marcus Valerius Martialis wrote:

Fifty million years ago this ant crawled up the trunk of a pinelike tree near the Baltic Sea. Here it accidentally became trapped in sticky resin, which preserved it even after the tree died and decayed. Such fossilized ants show almost as much detail as when they were alive.

FRANK M. CARPENTER, CAMBRIDGE, MASSACHUSETTS

While an ant walking about in Phaeton's shadow,
Resenous drops quietly enshrouded the fragile creature,
Look at it now, unnoticed it was while still living,
But through entombment transformed into a gem.

In ancient times, the people living near the shores of the Baltic Sea found large quantities of amber along the beaches. It was especially abundant after storms, having been washed up from the sea bed as are shells. Since it is rather light in weight, it is easily washed ashore. Because of its value, it entered into international trade channels and eventually became a royal monopoly. A total of many million pounds were harvested over a period of several centuries.

Now that we have learned something about this strange fossil resin that we call amber, let us return once again to the Oligocene forests where it had its origin. While it is definitely known to have been produced by pinelike trees, amber occurs in "pockets" along with fossil shark teeth, oyster shells, and crabs, all of which are obviously of marine origin. How did the amber get there? It is now the theory of geologists that the amber, being rather light in weight, was carried down to the sea by rushing streams and buried under silt along with the remains of various marine animals. Here it remained as the long, slow millenia passed, until man appeared on the scene and found it useful.

Deposits of amber have been found in several parts of the world, in addition to the Baltic region. These include Mexico, Sicily, Romania, Burma, Zanzibar, Indonesia, Philippine Islands, the United States, and Canada. Amber has been found at Coffee Bluff, Harden County, Tennessee, and on Nantucket Island, Massachusetts. The amber of the latter location contained ants, a fly, and some beetles. Deposits of amber found in Canada are older than those of the Baltic; they are of Cretaceous origin or about 100 million years old. Amber of a similar age has been found on the slopes of the Arctic Ocean near Wainwright, Alaska.

A large deposit of amber was found in the Dominican Republic and is of special interest, since it was first reported by Christopher Columbus during his second voyage to the West Indies. This amber was found

Ants of the amber forests. These ants lived in the ancient forests of pinelike trees that, millions of years ago, grew near the Baltic Sea. The drawings were made from specimens that became entrapped in the resin of the trees and were preserved. At the left is Prionomyrmex longiceps *which probably lived in trees where it was predaceous on insects. It was nearly half an inch long. At upper right is* Oecophylla brischkei *which apparently was red in color. It was less than half an inch long and its relatives are now found only in certain tropical areas where they use their larvae as sources of silk for "sewing" leaves together to build nests. The winged ant at lower right is a male* Erebomyrma antiqua. *Probably brown in color, these ants were small and the wingless workers had very tiny eyes. It seems probable that they were thief ants, living underground where they stole food from other ground-dwelling ants.*

sometime between September, 1494, and March, 1496. It occurs in the Monti Cristi Range *(Cordillera Septentrional)* and contains many insects, spiders, flowers, and leaves; it is believed to be of approximately the same age as that found in the Baltic.

While the best preserved fossil insects are those that were trapped in amber, numerous other fossil insects have been found in shales and clays in many parts of the world. When all these fossil insects are considered, they tell a long story of insect evolution reaching far back in time. A total of about 13,000 species of prehistoric insects have been described in scientific literature.

Having considered the manner in which amber was formed and the fact that many ants and other insects were trapped and preserved in it, let us now see what these ants from the far past have to tell us. They reveal a strange story of the ancient world when climates were largely tropical and when mountains were rising to form great mountain chains and when great forests flourished. Fifty million years is a long time to the human race, but these beautifully preserved ants prove that their ancestors of the Oligocene age differed very little from those that inhabit the world today. They looked about the same, and probably had similar habits. One of the commonest ants of the Baltic amber was a black mount-building species *(Formica fusca)*, but this same ant, little changed by time, is still common in Europe. There are at least eight species of ants found in Baltic amber that are identical to those living today. Whether or not their habits have really changed, we do not know. The fact remains that even though the world and most of its animals have changed greatly, the ants apparently have changed but little.

During the Oligocene period there were ants which sought out and protected aphids for their honeydew, just as do some kinds of modern ants. Both these ants and their aphid "cows" were trapped and preserved in the amber. These fossil ants also tell us that, even as today, ants of long ago had their parasites. Two ants *(Lasius schiefferdeckeri)* were found in amber with tiny, parasitic mites attached to their hind legs. We saw, in a previous chapter, how modern ants have many ant-loving beetles and other insects or "pets" living with them. We know from specimens found in amber that the ancient ants, too, had these

186

Posed on a twig of a female ginkgo tree is a Lasius *ant found preserved in Baltic amber. What is especially interesting is the small mite attached to the ant's hind leg. Similar mites often attach themselves to the legs and bodies of modern ants.*

"star boarders." There were tiny ant-loving beetles and other insects. It is probable also that some Oligocene ants had already developed the habit of enslaving other ants as do some modern kinds. One of the strangest things of all about ancient ants is that relating to an ant discovered in Baltic amber and named *Gesomyrmex*. Years later, it was found that this same ant still lives in Borneo! In this same tropical region are also found weaver ants (*Oecophylla*), but these ants once lived in the cool Baltic forests and they, too, became trapped in the sticky resin, thus furnishing additional proof that its climate was once warm and tropical.

As a result of our studies of these ancient ants we see that their legions have lived on down through time but little changed by the passing ages. Then, as now, their winged males and queens swarmed out of parent nests and flew away through the forests to establish colonies. They had their enemies and parasites and the ever-present problems of obtaining food.

187

Chapter 14

The Termite Clan

TERMITES ARE SOMETIMES called "white ants," which is unfortunate since they are not ants at all. Ants belong to the insect order Hymenoptera, and thus are closely related to wasps. Termites belong to the insect order Isoptera, which includes very ancient insects, even more ancient than the ants.

To those of us who live in cool climates, termites are pests that eat wood and thereby destroy our homes. But the true "kingdom of the termites" is that portion of the world which lies within the tropical zone. This is where most of them are found and where they build their largest and most elaborate nests.

While ants have hard, shell-like bodies, the bodies of termites, especially the soldier and worker castes, are pale and soft. In addition, their caste system differs from that found in ants. Worker ants and soldiers, you will recall, are all imperfect females. By contrast, termite workers and soldiers may be of either sex, and their societies are very complex. Termite reproductive castes are winged kings and queens which emerge from old nests at certain seasons and pair off. While hundreds of kings and queens may emerge from the parent nest during this swarming period, only a very few ever live to found colonies; the rest are destroyed by enemies.

Actually, mating of king and queen termites does not occur immediately; after pairing off, each queen and her king select a nesting site where they shed their wings, which break off along *fracture* or "breaking lines." Mating then occurs and, eventually, the queen begins laying eggs. These are the first steps in the founding of a new termite colony.

In such a young colony, the first eggs are cared for by the king and queen but, later, the eggs are cared for by workers. Termite eggs do

Newly emerged termite males and females have wings and eyes. After pairing off and establishing themselves in a chosen cavity in wood, they mate and sever their wings. The queen then becomes a mere layer-of-eggs and her abdomen gradually swells to relatively enormous proportions.

not hatch as quickly as do most insect eggs; usually from one to two months are required. Upon hatching, these eggs may produce individuals of several different kinds; some of them may develop into soldiers which have large heads and jaws in the case of our common subterrannean termite *(Reticulitermes)*. In others, the soldiers' heads are shaped like squirt guns and contain sticky or disagreeable substances which are squirted on ants or other enemies. These are called *nasutoid* soldiers and are found in tropical termites of several kinds. While soldier ants are always of the female sex, termite soldiers may be either male or female. Their function or work is the protection of the colony. When a termite nest is broken open, the soldiers station themselves at the openings to prevent the entry of enemies while the workers are busy repairing the damage. Apparently, termite soldiers fulfill their protective duties best within the nest. Termite workers usually toil in the darkness, but the workers of certain tropical termites leave their nests and go on foraging expeditions.

In most termites, the largest proportion of individuals in a colony is of the worker caste. These are the ones who eat wood, feed the young and the queen, build tunnels, and do other work. They are wingless and usually blind. Like the soldiers, they are sterile; that is,

189

These tropical termites (Nasutitermes) *have heads shaped like squirt guns. The nozzle extending from the front of this termite's head is used to squirt a disagreeable substance at ants to repel them. Ants are termites' greatest enemies.*

they do not mate or lay eggs. In truth, the workers, even though they do not lay eggs or mate, may be either males or females. In general, it may be said that when the soldiers are males, the workers are females, or the other way around.

In the case of ants, there is usually only one egg-laying queen. In the case of termites, however, there may be several "supplementary reproductives" or other male and female termites who can and do take the place of the king and queen.

Once the queen termite settles down to her egg-laying, she moves about but little. In fact, she becomes so swollen with eggs that she can only move with difficulty. While the queens of our native termites become only about half an inch long, those of some tropical kinds become enormous; they may be four or five inches in length and contain nearly 50,000 eggs. During her lifetime, such a queen may lay millions of eggs.

The above is the general, social structure of most termite colonies. It is obvious that their lives are quite complicated and it should be remembered, too, that the social structures of the various kinds of termites are not all the same.

One of the most remarkable things about termites is their method of digesting wood. Wood, as you may know, consists largely of *cellulose*, a very difficult substance for animals to digest, but many termites, including those here in our own country, have successfully solved this problem. Living within the hind intestines of these termites are numer-

190

Here are shown two winged termite "sex forms" and a wingless worker.

Eventually the termite queen's abdomen becomes so swollen with eggs that the original plates are stretched far apart and look like dark areas. This is the queen of the subterranean termite (Reticulitermes) found in the United States. The queens of some tropical termites measure more than three inches in length.

Termite workers are wingless and blind. They digest wood by means of protozoa (microscopic animals) which live in their intestines. At the lower left are seen two members of the soldier caste. They have large heads and jaws.

ous Protozoa or single-celled animals. While most Protozoa, such as *Paramecium*, live in ponds and similar places, those that inhabit the intestines of termites are completely dependent upon their hosts and cannot live anywhere else. These termite Protozoa, of which there are many kinds, have the ability to digest cellulose. The products of this digestion are then absorbed by the termites. These Protozoans are classified in the order Hypermastigida and, though most of them dwell in termites, a few kinds live in other insects.

While most termites obtain their nourishment from wood, others actually forage above ground during daylight hours to collect grass, leaves, and pine needles. Like the harvester ants, there are at least two kinds of termites *(Termes latericus* and *Eutermes trinervius)* in South Africa which collect seeds and store them in granaries. Others collect grass fragments for storage. In Ceylon, there is a termite *(Eutermes monoceros)* which forages in long files, like army ants. These foragers leave their nest about sunset and the soldiers line themselves up along the sides of the column as guards. These expeditions are made to collect lichen fragments which are fed to their young. These termites spend the entire night afield and it has been estimated that about 300,000 individuals take part.

Here in the United States are found two types of termites. Most common are the subterranean kinds *(Reticulitermes)*, which usually have their nests in damp ground and which often build tunnels or covered runways up into wooden structures above ground. This is the kind which causes the most damage to homes. However, these termites are rather easy to combat, since all that is needed is to make it impossible for them to reach the wooden timbers of a house by means of metal barriers. Their colonies can also be destroyed by insecticides. The other type of termite commonly found in the United States are the dry-wood termites *(Kalotermes)*. These termites establish their colonies in wood and do not require connection with moist soil. These latter termites are found only in the southern portions of our country.

As we noted previously, the tropical parts of the world are where termites have really come into their own. Some kinds build enormous earthen mounds, often as large as human residences. The material out of which these mounds are built consists of earth mixed with a secretion

Ground-living termites construct hollow tubes to connect their feeding places in wooden timbers with their underground nests. These hollow tubes are built of wood fragments cemented together.

Termite tubes are built from the inside. Here we see a worker cementing an addition to the lower end of a tube.

from the termites, which makes them almost waterproof. While many of these termite mounds are oval in form, others may be of unusual shape. The mounds of one termite *(Cubitermes)* are shaped like large mushrooms. In the case of the compass termite *(Amitermes meridianalis)* of Australia, the above-ground mounds are wedge-shaped and orientated so that the longest dimension always extends north and south. What the purpose of this is seems to be in doubt. Some authorities believe that the termites build their mounds in this way as a protection against the heat of the sun. By having the flat sides of the nests facing east and west, they are exposed to the full rays of the sun only during morning and afternoon. The fact remains, however, that they are always orientated thus and so are useful to bushrangers in telling direction.

While a number of different kinds of ants found in North and South America cultivate fungus or mushroom gardens in their underground nests, there are certain African termites which also have this habit. The fungus-growing termites *(Macrotermes natalensis)* chew up wood fragments and use this as a compost for growing the special fungus upon which they feed. However, unlike the fungus-growing ants, these termites reserve the fungus for their young and for their kings and queens. Mere workers must eat other food.

These same termites build what is probably the most remarkable nest used by any insect in the world. These nests, or *termitaries*, are more or less dome-shaped with raised ridges or vanes extending down over the sides. They are very large, often measuring sixteen feet tall and about the same in diameter.

It is the interior architecture of these nests, however, which is so remarkable. There is a large central nest cavity having numerous passages and chambers within which the termites live and grow their fungus. Millions of termites may occupy the nest. Just above this central nest area there is an open "attic" and, below it, an open "basement." Since the earthen walls surrounding this nest are thick and very hard, there is an accumulation of moisture and impure air within the nest chambers.

The fungus garden growing within the nest gives off both heat and moisture and uses up the oxygen in the air. It is estimated that such a large termite nest may use about 250 cubic feet of air a day. This air,

The compass termites (Amitermes meridionalis) of Australia build these tall, wedge-shaped mounds. Often as tall as fifteen feet, these mounds are always orientated north and south, probably to avoid the midday heat.

Here a termite soldier emerges from a tunnel in wood. If you look closely you can see a parasitic mite on its head.

of course, contains essential oxygen. Since these termite mounds are almost airtight, the inhabitants would soon die if there were no means of air purification. Moisture must also be eliminated and the nest cooled.

These remarkable termites have evolved an effective air-conditioning and air-purification system that is little short of ingenious. It works like this. Extending out of the "attic" are openings or ducts which extend into the ridges or vanes on the sides of the mound. Stale, heated air, rising from the central nest chambers, passes into these openings. Within the vanes, the ducts divide into smaller passages, all leading downward. These branching passages are quite near the outside surface of the mound, and moisture and heat filter out and the air is purified as it passes downward. Eventually, this purified air flows into the "basement" and upward again through the chambers of the central nest area. Studies have shown that temperatures within these termitaries are quite constant. Apparently, the termites regulate the temperature by opening and closing the openings into the cooling vanes, thus controlling the flow of air. No thermostat could do a more effective job of regulating temperature. Thus, the termites' living quarters are cooled, the air purified and the humidity lowered.

Like ants, termites have many enemies. At the time of swarming, a large percentage of the winged kings and queens are devoured by birds, lizards, and toads. Anteaters, in tropical countries, regularly break into their nests and capture them with their long, sticky tongues. Ants are the ancient enemies of termites and many kinds prey upon

A mount-building termite (Macrotermes natalensis) *of Africa constructs large earthen nests, often as high as sixteen feet. This nest is air-conditioned as shown in this diagram. Warm air, rising from the central nest chamber, passes out into cooling vanes through holes in the "attic." This humid air is purified and cooled as it passes downward through passages in the raised "vanes" or ridges on the sides of the mound. From here the purified air enters the "basement" and again rises through the central nest chamber.*

them. One of these is *Carebara*, a thief ant that lives in tropical termite nests. When the young termite queen leaves the parent nest on her wedding flight, the *Carebara* queen clings to her legs. Thus, when the termite queen and her king found their colony, the *Carebara* queen is also present and begins her own colony in the same place. The workers which the *Carebara* queen produces are very tiny; in fact, they are about a thousand times smaller than their queen! Their minute size enables them to move freely among the termites. Apparently, these tiny ants feed upon the young termites.

Again, like ants, termites have numerous "house guests." These are called *termitophiles*, a term meaning "termite-loving" and their relationships to their hosts are quite similar to those that live with ants. Among these star boarders are beetles, flies, silverfish insects, springtails, mites, and others.

A Selected Bibliography

For those who wish to delve further into the fascinating study of ants, the following publications will be found helpful:

Cook, Thomas W. *Ants of California.* Palo Alto, California: Pacific Books, 1953.

Creighton, W. S. *Ants of North America.* (Bulletin of the Museum of Comparative Zoology, Vol. 104) Cambridge, Massachusetts: Harvard University Press, 1950.

Crompton, John. *Ways of the Ant.* Boston, Massachusetts: Houghton Mifflin Co., 1954.

Goetsch, Wilhelm. *Ants.* Ann Arbor, Michigan: University of Michigan Press, 1957.

Gregg, Robert E. *Ants of Colorado.* Boulder, Colorado: University of Colorado Press, 1963.

Hutchins, Ross E. *Insects.* Englewood Cliffs, New Jersey: Prentice-Hall, Inc., 1966.

Larson, Mervin W. and Peggy. *All About Ants.* Cleveland, Ohio: World Publishing Co., 1965.

Michener, C. D. and M. H. *American Social Insects.* Princeton, New Jersey: D. Van Nostrand Co., 1951.

Smith, M. R. *House-infesting Ants of the Eastern United States.* United States Department of Agriculture Technical Bulletin, 1965.

Wheeler, W. M. *Ants, Their Structure, Development and Behavior.* New York, N. Y.: Columbia University Press, 1926.

Index

*Page numbers in **boldface** are those on which illustrations appear*

Aardvark, 179
Acrobatic ant, 31, **36**, 127
Alder aphid, 129, **130**
Amber, ants of, 180-187
Ambrosia beetle, 109
Amitermes, 194, **195**
Ammochaetae, **84**
Anatole, 131
Androeuryops, 64
Ant fungi, 96
Ant-lion, **175**, 176
Anteater, 179
Antennae, **17**, **19**, **55**
Ants
  ages of, 34
  antennae of, **17**, **19**, **55**
  beetle guests of, 167
  castes of, 6
  cocoons of, 31, **119**, **136**
  colors of, 30, 59
  during floods, **172**
  eggs of, 30, 59
  enemies of, 171-**175**
  eyes of, 20, **21**, **22**, **42**, 51
  feet of, **19**
  food of, 46, 47
  guests of, 158-170
  hearing in, 24
  in amber, **183**, **185**
  Japanese word for, **27**
  largest, **25**
  larval, 5, **6**, 7, **10**, **12**, 30, 31, 59, **61**, **68**, **80**, **156**
  legs of, 19, 20, **84**
  life histories of, 30-33
  males of, **21**, 33, **51**, 52
  number of, 28
  parasites of, **173**, 174
  pupal, **9**, **12**, 31

  queens of, **7**, **8**, 33, 61, 54
  smallest, **24**
  societies of, 11, 171
  soldiers of, 6, **51**, **52**, **53**, **55**, **56**, **139**, **140**, **141**
  sound making by, 24, 45
  stings of, **24**, **33**, 34
  strength of, **82**, 93
  structure of, 15, 16, 17, 18-20
  subfamilies of, 34-38
  workers of, 5, 32, 33, **53**
Anuraphis, 126
Argentine ant, **35**, 38
Aristida grass, 75
Armadillo, **179**
Army ants, **19**, 21, 50
  antennae of, **19**
  black, **64**
  daily cycle of, 57
  daily raids of, 59
  during floods, **172**
  eggs of, 59
  feet of, **19**
  food of, 56, 57, 63
  guests of, **163**
  hunting raids of, 57, 59
  in United States, **65**
  larvae of, 59, **61**
  life cycle of, 59, **61**
  marches of, 56, 57, 67, 68, 69
  myrmecophiles of, 63, 64, **163**
  nest cluster of, **60**
  queen, **7**, **8**, 33, 59
  soldier, **55**, **56**, **58**, **62**, **63**
  worker, **58**
Arthropoda, 15
Atelura, 166
Atemeles, **168**, 169

Atta, 11, **16**, 24, **32**, **36**, 37, 87
  colony founding by, 101
  fungus gardens of, **88**, 91, **92**, **95**, 96,
    97, 98, 103
  humidity control by, 97
  jaws of, **92**
  queen, **97**, **101**
  sounds made by, 93, 96
  trails of, 87, **88**, 89
  underground nests of, **90**, 91
Attaphila, **161**, 162
Azteca, **144**, 145, 149, **151**, 152, 154

Baltic amber, 182, **183**, 184-187
Barro Colorado Island, 54
Bates, Henry Walter, 54
Beetle, rove, **163**
Belt, Thomas, 149
Beltian bodies, 149, **150**
Bernstein (Burnsteyn), 181, 182
Bothriomyrmex, 132
Bromatia, 98, **99**
Bulldog ant, 18, **21**, **33**, 34, 41, **42**, **43**,
    44, **49**
Bull-horn acacia, **35**, 36, **145**, **146**, **147**,
    148, 149, **150**, **153**
Butterfly guest, 166

Calodixia, 64
Camponotus, **4**, **7**, **8**, **10**, 14, **37**, 38, 48,
    49, 122, 130, 142, 154, 159, **182**
Carebara, 198
Carpenter ant, **4**, **7**, **8**, **10**, 14, 48, 49, 130
  larva of, **10**
Castes, production of, 33
Cecropia tree, **151**
Chitin, 182
Claviger, 168
Cockroach, **161**
Cocoons, 31, 34, **61**, **119**, **136**
Colobopsis, 33, **37**, 138, **139**, **140**, **141**
Colony founding, 7-9
Communication, **4**
Compass termite, 194
Compound eye, 20
Coquillettia, 164
Cornfield ant, 126
Coxa, 20
Cremastochilus, 167
Crematogaster, 31, 36, 37, **127**, 144
  in resin, **182**
  nests of, 145
Cricket, **159**, **160**
Cryptocerus, **143**

Cubitermes, 194
Cyphomyrmex, 109

Daceton, **40**
Dasypus, **179**
Dermaptera, 2
Dinarda, 164, 170
Dinergate, 33
Dinoponera, **25**, **35**
Dolichoderinae, **35**, 37, 123
Dorylinae, 34, **35**, 39, 50, 123
Dorylus, 23, 34, **35**, 50, 54, **66**, 163
Dorymyrmex, 171
Driver ants, 21, **22**, **35**, 50, **51**
  eyes of, **21**
  food of, 66, 68
  guests of, 163
  jaws of, **67**
  larva of, **68**
  males of, **21**, **51**, **52**
  marches of, **66**, 67
  pupae of, **69**
  queen of, 59
  soldier of, **51**, **52**, **53**, 54
  worker of, **53**, **58**

Earwig, 2
Eciton, **18**, **19**, **23**, 34, **35**, 50, 54, 56, 65
  colony size, 30
  guests of, **163**
  hunting raids of, 57, 59
Ectatomma, **35**
Eggs, 6, 30, 31, 33
  army ant, 59, **61**
  harvester ant, 85, 86
  termite, 188-190
Elektron, 182
Erebomyrma, **185**
Eutermes, 192

Feniseca, 129
Fire ant, **29**, 37, **46**, **47**, **128**
  guests of, **159**
  parasites of, 173
Formica, 9, 13, 30, 34, **37**, 38, 47, **48**,
    132, **133**, **134**, **136**, 137, 186
  enemies of, 173
  guests of, 162
Formicinae, **37**, 38, 123
Formicoxenus, 173
Fungus gardens, **88**, **90**, 91, **92**, **95**, 96,
    97, **99**, **101**, 102, **104**, **106**, 109
Fustiger, **167**

Garden of the Gods, **112**, 114
Gesomyrmex, 187
Giant anteater, 179
Ginkgo, **187**

Harpegnathus, 14, 46
Harvester ants, 26, 27, **28**, 29, 33, 82
  daily routine of, 84, 85
  enemies of, 171, 172, **174**
  food of, 22, 70, 80
  grain bins of, **75**
  guests of, **159**, **160**
  kinds of, 74
  larvae of, **80**
  nests of, **73**, 74, 76, **77**, **78**, **79**, **80**, 83
  pupae of, **9**, **80**
  queen of, **79**
  seed-gathering by, 71, 72, **86**
  southeastern, 80
  stings of, 29
  strength of, **82**
  swarming of, 85
  western, 29, **73**
Hetaerius, 165
Hister beetle, 164, 165
Holcaspis, 114
Honey ants, **37**, 110, **112**
  American, 38
  Australian, 38, 122
  cocoons of, **119**
  larvae of, **119**
  nests of, 113, **114**, **117**
Honeydew, 114, **115**, 118, 123, 125, **126**
Horace, 26
Horned lizard, **174**
Hunting ants, 39-47

Iridomyrmex, **35**, 38

Jumping ants, 46

Kalotermes, 192
Kelep ant, **35**
King Solomon, 23, 26, 27

Labidus, **64**
Larvae, 5, 6
  army ant, 59, **61**
  carpenter ant, **10**
  driver ant, **68**
  harvester ant, **6**, **80**
  honey ant, **119**
  tailor ant, **155**, **156**, 157
Lasius, 34, 38, 126, **187**

Leaf-cutting ants, 11, **16**, 24, **32**, **36**, 87-104
  colony founding by, 102
  fungus gardens of, 91, **92**, **95**, 96-98, 103
  guest of, **161**
  humidity control by, 97
  loads carried by, 93, **94**, **95**
  sounds made by, 24, 93, 96
  trails of, **88**
  underground chambers of, **90**, 91
  workers of, 32, **101**
Leptalea, 36, 149
Leptaleinae, **35**, 36
Leptogenys, 34
Leptothorax, 173
Liphyra, 166
Lomechusa, **168**-170
Lubbock, Sir John, 34
Lycaena, 129, 131

McCook, Henry C., 113
Macrogate, 32
Macromischa, 142, **144**
Macrotermes, 194, 196, **197**
Male ants, 6, 33
  army ant, **21**, 22
  driver ant, **21**, **51**, **52**
Mata ant, **35**
Mealybug, **125**, **128**, 144
Mecistorhinus, **1**, 2
Megalotomus, **164**
Megaponera, 45
Meloporus, 38
Messor, 26, 37, 70, **71**, 72
Metopina, 174
Microdon, 167
Microgate, 32
Moellerius, 109
Monomorium, **12**
Mosaic vision, 20
Mound-building ant, **37**
Müllerian bodies, **151**
Mycetosoritis, 109
Myrmarachne, 164
Myrmecia, 14, 18, **21**, **33**, 34, 36, 41, **42**, **43**, **44**, **49**, **168**, 173
Myrmecinae, **36**, 37
Myrmecocystus, **37**, 38, **112**, 122
Myrmecophaga, 179
Myrmecophila, **159**
Myrmecophile, 158, **159**-170

Nasutitermes, 190

Nectaries, **147**, 148
Neoponera, 46

Oak galls, 114, **115**
Oecophylla, 30, **37**, 38, 154, 155, **156**, 157, **185**, 187
Odontomachus, 14, **44**, **45**
Oligocene, 180, 181, **185**, 186, 187

Pachycondyla, 174
Panama Canal Zone, 54
Pangolin, 179
Parasol ant, 37
Partridge pea, **153**
Pemphigus, 129, **130**
Pentatomid, 2
Pheidole, 30, **36**, 70, 72, 170, 172
Pheidoloxenus, **170**
Pinites, 181
Pitcher plant, **177**
Plagiolepis, 122
Plant lice, **125**, **143**
Pogonomyrmex, 22, **28**, 33, 37, 46, 70, 71, 73
    enemies of, 171, 172
    miller caste of, 27
    nests of, **73**, 74, 76, **77**, **78**, **79**, **80**
    pupae of, **9**
    queen, **79**
    species of, 74
Polyergus, **37**, 38
Polymorphism, 32, 54
Polyrhachis, 154, **155**
Ponera, **36**, 41, 45
Ponerinae, 34, **35**, 36, 41, 123
Prenolepis, **111**, 112
Prionomyrmex, **185**
Protozoa, 191, 192
Pselaphidae, **167**
Pseudogyne, 32
Pseudomyrma, **35**, 36, **145**, **146**, 148-**150**
Ptilocerus, 170
Pupae, 31, 34
    army ant, 59
    driver ant, **69**
    harvester ant, **9**, **80**
    little black ant, **12**

Queen, 6
    army ant, **7**, **8**, 33, 54, 59, 61
    carpenter ant, **4**, **7**
    driver ant, 59
    harvester ant, **79**

leaf-cutting ant, **97**, **101**
termite, 188, **189**, **191**
    Trachymyrmex, **101**

Replete, 116, **118**, **119**, 120, **121**
Reticulitermes, 189, 192
Robber ant, 38
Rove beetle, 164

Sauba ant, 109
Scent trails, 22, 23, **47**
Schneirla, T. C., 56
Sclerioderma, **13**
Shampoo ant, 173
Silverfish, **166**
Slave-making ant, 37, 38, 132, **133**, 134-137
Smithistruma, 171
Social habits, 1-14
Soldiers, 6
    army ant, **18**, **23**, 54, **55**, **56**, **58**, **62**, **63**
    driver ant, **51**, **52**, **53**, 54, **55**, **56**
    termite, 189, **191**, **196**
    trap-door ant, **139**, **140**, **141**
Solenopsis, 29, 30, 36, 37, 46, 70, 171, **173**
Solomon's ant, **71**, 72
Sounds, 24, 45
Spiders, 164
Stigmatomma, 41, 45
Stings, **29**, **33**, 34, 41, **44**
Strumigenys, **24**, 40
Stylogaster, 64
Succinic acid, 181
Succinite, 181
Succinosis, 181
Symbiosis, 123
Synemosyna, 164
Syrphid fly, 167

Tailor ants, 30, 38, **155**, **156**
Tapinoma, **35**, 38, 132, 133
Tarsi, 20
Termes, 192
Termites, 45, 188
    air-conditioning in, 194, 196, **197**
    castes of, 189-**191**
    compass, 194, **195**
    damage by, 192
    eggs of, 188-190
    enemies of, 190, **196**, 197, 198
    fungus growing by, 194, **195**, 196, **197**
    guests of, 198
    kings of, 188, **189**

204

parasites of, **196**
protozoa of, 191, 192
queens of, 188, **189**, **191**
seed collecting by, 192
sexes of, 189
soldiers of, 189, **191**, **196**
tropical, 192
tunnels of, **193**
workers of, 188, 191, **193**
Termitophiles, 198
Thief ant, 171, 172
Tibia, 20
Tic-ant, **45**
Tiger beetles, **176**
Trachymyrmex, 105-109
  fungus garden of, **99**, **102**, **104**, **106**, **109**
  nest of, **102**
  queen of, **101**
Trap-door ant, **37**, 138, **139**
Trochanter, 20
Trophallaxis, 5

Uropod mite, **173**

Venus-flytrap, 177, **178**
Virgil, 26

Wanderer butterfly, 129
Warrior ant, 50-69
"White ants," 188
Wood ant, 9
Woodpeckers, 174
Workers, 8, 9, 33, 34
  army ant, **54**, **58**
  driver ant, **53**, **58**
  leaf-cutting ant, 32, **101**
  termite, 188, **191**, 193
  Trachymyrmex, **105**, **107**, **108**
  trap-door ant, 141

Xendusa, 168

Yellowjacket, **2**

The Author—Photographer

Entomologist Ross E. Hutchins is also an expert nature photographer, and this combination of interests has resulted in more than thirty years of studying, photographing and writing about insects, plants, animals and birds. Born in Montana, he grew up on a cattle ranch near Yellowstone Park. At Montana State College he majored in biological sciences and later he received his Ph.D. in zoology and entomology from Iowa State College.

Dr. Hutchins' articles and pictures of natural history subjects have appeared in encyclopedias, books and magazines, among them *National Geographic, Life* and *Natural History,* as well as such European publications as *Sie und Er, La Vie des Bêtes* and *Sciences et Avenir.* His most recent books in the juvenile field include PLANTS WITHOUT LEAVES, CADDIS INSECTS, THE AMAZING SEEDS, and the companion volumes, THIS IS A LEAF, THIS IS A FLOWER, and THIS IS A TREE. All are noted for their remarkable close-up photographs by the author.

Ross Hutchins lives in Mississippi where he is Director of the State Plant Board of Mississippi and Professor of Entomology at Mississippi State University. He is listed in WHO'S WHO and AMERICAN MEN OF SCIENCE.